NEW DIMENSIONS IN ECONOMIC ANALYSIS OF LEGAL ISSUES:

The Appropriate Regulatory Balance of Antitrust Law in the Context of the Technological Innovation

Abstract

The role of Empirical study in legal decision, even in the rule making, was increased by the economic development with the occurrence of economic realism. The incensement of economic implication of the law, without exception, impacted to the court's ruling in the antitrust case and the antitrust law-making itself. Now it is one of the common way, court use concepts and theories developed by economists and weaves economic concepts into decisions to support their result.

The classical perspective of economic theories regarding antitrust law was start from early theorist Adam Smith in 1776, even it denied the economic implication. Through this dissertation, it was examined several modern economic theories along with Posner's economic implication of antitrust law. Economic Realism, Neo-classical synthesis, and Chicago School's economic view on antitrust law also was covered briefly.

In addition, to analyze the substantial implication of economic theories, it should be back to Jefferson and Hamilton's contrasting views on governance. Because it is the same vein with current debates on the antitrust law where we should put the value on protectionism for equality-enhancing opportunities or efficiency-enhancing competitions. Jefferson urged a deconcentrated society and government, one that valued independent decision-making and equality-enhancing opportunities for small, local business. Control of economic concentrations of industrial power was central to Jeffersonian populism. Hamilton, on the other hand, feared that decentralization might interfere with the goal of efficiency. He was an exponent of a strong national government, particularly central control over financial and economic issues and institutions.

In the same vein, many commentators on the patent-antitrust intersection frame the issue as raising an inherent tension because antitrust aims to protect competition, whereas patent law creates monopolies that aim to eliminate competition in order to reward invention. However, it is doubtable whether the conflict is not a real conflict that we generally or conceptually had been long-accepted. Ultimately, IP confliction issues with Antirust case should be analysis in the same line with the regular antitrust case analysis. It is not the matter of confliction between to protect competition and to eliminate competition, but the matter of alteration of legal application methodology or legal doctrine.

Finally, back to the role of Empirical study in legal decision, the alteration of legal methodology or doctrine specially in the antitrust law that the tendency of change of empirical data analyses and economic implications, is unavoidable. Economic data analysis can be another barrier for the party who has less availability to conduct expense data analyzing to support or to rebut the argument in the court. Thus, government should put resources or efforts to reduce the barriers that are producing unfair justice and inequalities.

Table of Contents

Introduction

In the early stage of development, economists originally shunned or were indifferent towards antitrust policy, and they did not play a central role in the legislative debates of the Sherman Act.

However, the economic implication and role of empirical study in legal decisions, even in the rule making procedures, was increased by the economic development with the occurrence of economic realism[1]. The incensement of economic implication of the law, without exception, impacted to the court's ruling in the antitrust case and the antitrust law-making itself. Now, as one of the common way, court uses concepts and theories developed by economists and weaves economic concepts into decisions to support their result.

For instance, up to World War I, the economist played virtually no role in shaping antitrust policy. The main reason for this was a paucity of empirical studies upon which to base policy judgment. However, the appearance in the 1920's of a number of industry and firm studies filled this gap. In addition, in the 1930's, the most significant developments in economic thought occurred in the body of work known as "economic realism.[2]" In different works, Joan Robinson and Edward Chamberlin ushered in economic realism by focusing on market conditions between the poles of pure competition and pure monopoly.[3] They noted that in the real world, most industries are imperfectly competitive, and firms possess varying degrees of market power[4]. One

---

[1] *See generally*, STEVE FLEETWOOD, CRITICAL REALISM IN ECONOMIC: DEVELOPMENT AND DEBATE (1999).
[2] *Id.*
[3] *See generally*, Frank M. *Machovec, Mises, Monopoly, and the Market Process*, 19 Cato J. 247, 258 (1999).
[4] *Id.*

of the most important characteristics of imperfect or monopolistic competition is that the fewer the firms competing in a market, the greater the tendency for mutually interdependent conduct.[5]

However, economists growingly joined the debate as to the economic implications of antitrust. Now, courts routinely use concepts and theories developed by economists and weave economic concepts into decisions to support their results. The premise of antitrust is that some industries contributes best to overall social welfare if they are competitive.

Thus, my overall thesis will be an investigation of the following questions: what is the best economic and legal solution to reward innovation given the circumstance that antitrust law has become increasingly intertwined with intellectual property rights? What role should law play in dealing with the combined issues of antitrust and intellectual property rights? For example, when should a party be allowed to acquire a monopoly through the accumulation of patent rights? On the other hand, when should antitrust laws be applied to specific activities involving intellectual property rights that create market power? More broadly, what possible resolution of the conflict between domestic regulation and international jurisprudence would result in minimum economic loss from this conflict?

To examine the answer to those questions, I will discuss the traditional concept of antitrust laws with analysis of the American antitrust legal system. Specially, it focuses on the American antitrust laws, such as Sharman Act, Clayton Act, Robinson Patman Act, and the Federal Trade Commission Act. Additionally, I will discuss the Enforcement of the antitrust laws, as well. In this part of discussion, analysis of statutory structures among the American antitrust laws is included.

---

[5] *Id.*

In the next chapter, to find out the answers to my research questions under American antitrust law and America's industrial structures, it also analyzes the court's approaches which have changed throughout time. So far, throughout the court's ruling, the application of antitrust law in America has comingled with those Acts. It also has changing the application of the 'per se' rule and 'the rule of reasons.' It has changed even on similar issues. The 'Per se Rule' is "the judicial principle that a trade practice violates the Sherman Act simply if the practice is a restraint of trade, regardless of whether it actually harms anyone"[6] and 'Rule of Reason' is "the judicial doctrine holding that a trade practice violates the Sherman Act only if the practice is on unreasonable restraint of trade, based on the totality of economic circumstances."[7]

As another part of the analysis in this thesis, I will discuss historical economic theories and I will also economically analyzes the antitrust law. This step is significant because an analysis of antitrust history and economics is essential to understanding law's actual operation- its failures and success.

American courts have adopted various rationales for changing their decisions. Increasingly, it relies on economic theories and sometimes it borrows economic assumptions to rationalize its decisions. However, the early stage of American antitrust law was not characterized by economic theories and they literally denies its economic implication.

The classical perspective of economic theories regarding antitrust law start from early theorist Adam Smith in 1776, even it denies the economic implication.[8] This dissertation examines several modern economic theories along with Posner's economic implication of antitrust law.

---

[6] US LEGAL, Inc., https://definitions.uslegal.com/p/per-se-rule/ (last visited Jan. 5. 2017).
[7] US LEGAL, Inc., https://definitions.uslegal.com/r/rule-of-reason/ (last visited Jan. 5. 2017).
[8] ADAM SMITH, JONATHAN B. WIGHT: AN INQUIRY INTO THE NATURE AND CAUSES OF THE WEALTH OF NATIONS (2007).

Economic Realism, Neo-classical Synthesis, and Chicago School's economic view on antitrust law also will be covered briefly. In addition to economic theoretical inquiry, it analyzes the real market application of the economic theories under the American antitrust law.

To analyze the substantial implication of economic theories, it discusses the genesis of the antitrust debate. The genesis of the antitrust debate predates the first antitrust statute, the Sherman Act of 1890. The debate is as old as Jefferson and Hamilton's contrasting views on governance.[9] Jefferson urged a deconcentrated society and government, one that valued independent decision-making and equality-enhancing opportunities for small, local businesses.[10] Control of economic concentrations of industrial power was central to Jeffersonian populism.[11] Hamilton, on the other hand, feared that decentralization might interfere with the goal of efficiency.[12] He was an exponent of a strong national government, particularly central control over financial and economic issues and institutions.[13]

Even if you leave these two themes out of the discussion, today, there is agreement that the antitrust laws were written foremost to encourage competition, not the competitors. Basically, the continuing debate over whether the goal of promoting competition was rooted in concern over allocative efficiency or the distribution of wealth is not likely to be resolved soon. In the relationship between antitrust law and economics, economists tend to make cost and benefit arguments in support of legal rules that they find to be efficient and against legal rules that they find to be inefficient.

---

[9] SAUL CORNELL, THE OTHER FOUNDERS: ANTI-FEDERALISM AND THE DISSENTING TRADITION IN AMERICA, 179-1828 (1999).
[10] *Id.*
[11] *Id.*
[12] *Id.*
[13] *Id.*

In the last part of my thesis, I will reconcile the confliction between IP and Antitrust law. Many commentators on the patent-antitrust intersection frame the issue as raising an inherent tension because antitrust aims to protect competition, whereas patent law creates monopolies that aim to eliminate competition in order to reward invention. Under this framing, adjudicators must reconcile this tension as best they can by determining which restraints desirably increase the reward the patent holder gets for is innovation and whether that benefit offsets any anticompetitive effect. This approach presumes that patent rights merit special treatment compared to other property rights.

However, the difficulties are that which patent rewards are necessary to incentivize is unclear, and it is even less clear what incentive effect comes from any incremental increase in reward that would be produced by restraints associated with patents. Thus, it emphasizes how important IP and antitrust laws are to economic growth as well. This is a difficult issue to resolve both theoretically and empirically. Also, the evidence of the effect of both is mixed.

The United States is the leading country in terms of dealing with the intersection of IP and Antitrust law. American antitrust law guidelines dealing with the intersection of IP and Antitrust law have largely been followed in Europe, Australia, etc. The situation in Korea is not different from those countries that are adopting significant portions of American approaches in that area of law.

However, the question is whether or not these dealings are appropriate to reconcile the confliction between IP and Antitrust law. To find out the answer, it tries economic approaches regard to the confliction between IP and Antitrust with the introduce of modern economists' economic implication on the issues. It includes William Baxter, Ward Bowman, and Louise Kaplow.

Chapter I. General Perspectives on American Antitrust Law

1. Overview of Major Federal Antitrust Laws and the Enforcement

In the years after the Civil War, important parts of the American economy came to be dominated by large combinations of capital organized in the form of trust to avoid state laws restricting the size of corporations.[14] One of the most visible of these trusts was the 'Standard Oil Trust' organized by John D. Rockefeller.[15] By 1890, the public had come to believe that the market power of these trusts was leading to higher enforcement process and the unnecessary destruction of small business.[16] Thus, the 'Sherman Act[17]' was enacted by the United States Congress in 1890.[18] Its original name was based on its focus on the trusts, but the name antitrust is now used generally to describe any law that is intended to enhance competition. The federal antitrust laws also include the Clayton Act[19], the Robinson Patman Act[20] and the Federal Trade Commission Act[21]. In addition, each state has its own set of antitrust laws.

The history of Antitrust Laws started with the Sherman Antitrust Act. The Sherman Antitrust Act was enforced by the Attorney General from the time of its passage in 1890 until the

---

[14] *See generally*, IDA M. TARBELL, THE HISTORY OF THE STANDARD OIL COMPANY/IDA M. TARBELL; BRIEFER VERSION EDITED BY DAVID M. CHALMERS (2003).
[15] *Id.*
[16] *Id.*
[17] Pub. L. No. 94-435, Title 3, Sec. 305(a), 90 Stat. 1383 at p. 1397
[18] *See* William L. Letwin, Congress and the Sherman Antitrust Law: 1887-1890, 23 U.Chi.L.Rev 221 (1956)
[19] Pub.L. 63–212, 38 Stat. 730, enacted October 15, 1914, codified at 15 U.S.C. §§ 12–27, 29 U.S.C. §§ 52–53
[20] Pub. L. No. 74-692, 49 Stat. 1526 (codified at 15 U.S.C. § 13).
[21] 15 U.S.C. §§ 41-58

office of the Assistant to the Attorney General was established in 1903 during the administration

of President Theodore Roosevelt and Attorney General Philander Knox.[22]

The Assistant to the Attorney General handled antitrust matters from 1903 until 1933.

During this time, on October 15, 1914, the Clayton Act was enacted.[23]

In 1933, under the administration of President Franklin D. Roosevelt and Attorney

General Homer S. Cummings, the Antitrust Division was established, and Harold M. Stephens

was appointed the first Assistant Attorney General in charge of the Antitrust Division.[24]

A. The Sherman Act

The Sherman Antitrust Act has stood, since 1890, as the principal law expressing our

national commitment to a free market economy in which competition free from private and

governmental restraints leads to the best results for consumers[25]. Congress felt so strongly about

this commitment that there was only one vote against the Act.[26]

The Sherman Act outlaws all contracts, combinations, and conspiracies that unreasonably

restrain interstate and foreign trade. This includes agreements among competitors to fix prices,

rig bids, and allocate customers. The Sherman Act also makes it a crime to monopolize any part

---

[22] See *supra* 2.

[23] Ramirez, Carlos D., and Christian Eigen-Zucchi. "Understanding the Clayton Act of 1914: An analysis of the interest group hypothesis." Public Choice 106.1-2 (2001).

[24] Sullivan, E. Thomas. "The Antitrust Division as a Regulatory Agency: An Enforcement Policy in Transition." Wash. ULQ 64 (1986): 997.

[25] Bork, Robert H. "Legislative intent and the policy of the Sherman Act." The Journal of Law and Economics 9 (1966): 7-48.

[26] See *supra* 2.

of interstate commerce. An unlawful monopoly exists when only one firm controls the market for a product or service, and it has obtained that market power, not because its product or service is superior to others, but by suppressing competition with anticompetitive conduct. The Act is not violated simply when one firm's vigorous competition and lower prices take sales from its less efficient competitors—that is competition working properly.

The Sherman Act violations involving agreements between competitors usually are punished as criminal felonies. The Department of Justice alone is empowered to bring criminal prosecutions under the Sherman Act. Individual violators can be fined up to $1 million and sentenced to up to 10 years in Federal prison for each offense, and corporations can be fined up to $100 million for each offense. Under some circumstances, the maximum fines can go even higher than the Sherman Act maximums to twice the gain or loss involved.[27]

Sherman Act section 1 prohibits every "contract, combination in the form of trust or otherwise, or conspiracy in result of trade or commerce." Ironically, Section 1 is directed at activities involving two or more actors. Section 2 makes it illegal to monopolize, or attempt to monopolize or combine or conspire to monopolize. Section 2 is primarily directed at unilateral conduct involving one actor. As it is mentioned before, violation of the Sherman Act is a felony, punishable by fines and prison terms. Persons injured by reason of a violation of the Sherman Act can recover three times their actual damages, plus attorneys' fees. Future violations can be enjoined and injunctions can be issued to undo the harm of illegal activities. A contract entered into in violation of the Sherman Act can be avoided. The prohibitions of the Sherman Act are very general and reflect common law principles. Congress expected that courts would use the

---

[27] See *supra* 24.

general prohibitions in the Sherman Act to prohibit specific conduct leading to the evils it sought to eliminate. The Sherman Act therefore can be seen as enabling a common law of competition. At least some of those supporting the Sherman Act saw the preservation of small business units as a goal in and of itself, regardless of any effect on prices. Over time, that goal has been reflected in some Supreme Court decisions interpreting the Sherman Act. Today, the Sherman Act is seen almost entirely as promoting consumer welfare, and protecting competition, not competitors.[28]

A violation of Section 1 requires some kind of combined activity, such as an agreement, among otherwise independent entities, some restraint of trade resulting from that agreement, and an adverse effect on interstate commerce. Today, virtually all commercial activity has some effect on interstate commerce. Therefore, the focus is usually on the existence of agreements that restrain trade. Despite the different terms used to describe the actions prohibited by Section 1, the focus is always on an agreement or understanding between two or more parties that is intended to result either in a change in their behavior or some restrictions on future changes. The necessary agreement can be in writing or entirely oral. In addition, the necessary agreement can be found in conduct. The premise of the Sherman Act is that the overall welfare of society is improved by the independent action of multiple actors. Restriction of actors that are not independent is therefore not a target of the Sherman Act. The Sherman Act also does not apply to 'intra-enterprise conspiracies'[29] between a parent and a controlled subsidiary. There is no agreement if independent actors each choose to do the same thing without agreeing to restrictions on their freedom. Such behavior is called 'conscious parallelism' and it is not illegal because

---

[28] Flynn, John J. "Rethinking Sherman Act Section 1 Analysis: Three Proposals for Reducing the Chaos." Antitrust Law Journal 49.4 (1980).
[29] *Id.*

there is no agreement. In a concentrated market, conscious parallelism can lead to oligopolistic behavior. Under the law of contract, an enforceable agreement requires a meeting of the minds to be enforceable and coercion makes an agreement void. However, an illegal agreement under the Sherman Act can be formed through coercion. In 1920, the Supreme Court held that a dealer that continues to follow a manufacturer's policy to avoid being terminated has not entered into an agreement with that manufacturer.[30] This so-called 'Colgate Doctrine' has befuddled people, because it appears to lead to the same result as an agreement.[31] But the doctrine continues to provide a defense in many Sherman Act cases. To avoid charges of coercion, manufactures often couch their desires in terms of suggestions or recommendations, such as a manufacturers' suggested retail price. So long as the manufacturer avoids coercion and limits its discussions with the dealer to persuasion, the dealer's decision to follow the manufacturer's recommendations does not create an agreement. There is no express attempt prohibition in Section 1 and the courts have held there is no penalty under Section 1 for an unsuccessful effort to obtain an illegal agreement. Soliciting an illegal agreement is therefore not a violation of Section 1. However, solicitation of an illegal agreement could be a violation of Section 2 as attempted monopolization under certain circumstances.[32]

In the Supreme Court decision, Justice Brandeis recognized that the purpose of every agreement involving trade is to restrain the parties' actions, but not all agreements are illegal under the Sherman Act. So he announced the 'Rule of Reason,' under which agreements

---

[30] United States v. A. Schrader's Son, 252 US 85 (1920).
[31] Levi, Edward H. "The Parke, Davis-Colgate Doctrine: The Ban on Resale Price Maintenance." The Supreme Court Review 1960 (1960).
[32] *Id* at 12.

restraining trade are illegal under the Sherman Act only if they are unreasonable because their detrimental effects on competition, as measured in a relevant market, outweigh their benefits. [33]

Over the years, some types of agreements have been determined to have such seriously detrimental effects on competition and so little redeeming virtue that they are deemed illegal *per se*. For such agreements, adverse effects in a relevant market need not be proven and defenses or excuses for the agreements are allowed. Courts, more recently, have developed an intermediate mode of analysis, in-between the Rule of Reason and *per se* illegal, that is typically called "quick look." Under the quick look analysis, the anticompetitive harm is presumed, but a defense based on pro-competitive benefits is allowed. The quick look analysis tends to be used most often with not-for-profit organizations. [34]

In a series of cases, the Supreme Court held that agreements that seek aid from the government are not violations of the Sherman Act, even if the intent is to harm a competitor. Under this 'Noerr-Pennington Doctrine,' competitors can collectively seek zoning restrictions, legislative action, safety standards, etc. even if the action is directed against one or more of their competitors, so long as the action is not a sham. The Noerr-Pennington privilege to petition the government is lost if the activity is deemed to be a sham, intended only to harm the competitor through the process of responding to governmental action. To be a sham, the action must be objectively baseless, having no chance of success, and specifically intended to harm the competitor. [35]

---

[33] Posner, Richard A. "The rule of reason and the economic approach: Reflections on the Sylvania decision." The University of Chicago Law Review 45.1 (1977).

[34] Bork, Robert H. "The Rule of Reason and the Per Se Concept: Price Fixing and Market Division." The Yale Law Journal 74.5 (1965), Beckner, C. Frederick, and Steven C. Salop. "Decision theory and antitrust rules." Antitrust Law Journal 67.1 (1999).

[35] Fischel, Daniel R. "Antitrust Liability for Attempts to Influence Government Action: The Basis and Limits of the Noerr-Pennington Doctrine." The University of Chicago Law Review 45.1 (1977).

B. The Clayton Act

The Clayton Act is a civil statute (carrying no criminal penalties) that was passed in 1914 and significantly amended in 1950. The Clayton Act prohibits mergers or acquisitions that are likely to lessen competition. Under the Act, the Government challenges those mergers that a careful economic analysis shows are likely to increase prices to consumers. All persons considering a merger or acquisition above a certain size must notify both the Antitrust Division and the Federal Trade Commission. The Act also prohibits other business practices that under certain circumstances may harm competition.[36]

In 1914, Congress was concerned that the courts were not being sufficiently aggressive in enforcing Section 1 of the Sherman Act against certain types of conduct they thought were harming the economy.[37] For instance, there are tying cases involving commodities, exclusive dealing involving commodities, and mergers. As a result, Congress enacted the Clayton Act, which lowered the threshold of competitive injury needed for a violation.

To reach conduct deemed objectionable before it has actually harmed competition, the Clayton Act outlaws acts that "may be to substantially lessen competition."[38] Potentially harmful acts can be 'nipped in the bud' before damage actually occurs. Applying this standard, the courts began finding violations when relatively little market power was involved and then began applying the same standard to Section 1 claims that do not require that commodities be involved.

---

[36] See *supra* 22.
[37] See *supra* 17.
[38] See *supra* 22.

In addition, under Section 4 of the Clayton Act, persons injured by reason of a violation of the antitrust laws can recover three times their actual damages, plus their attorney's fees. Some people who can show an actual injury are not allowed to bring suit because they are too remote from the injury and therefore lack standing. For instance, only those who purchase directly from price fixers are allowed to sue to recover based on anti-competitive prices. Private plaintiffs must show that that aspect of the conduct that created the violation, called antitrust injury, injured them. In the merger cases, since a merger is rendered illegal because of the threat of high prices, competitors who claim that a merger harmed them because it reduced prices cannot recover because they lack antitrust injury. Similarly, competitors harmed by an agreement to set prices at low levels cannot recover if the prices are above cost.[39]

C. Robinson Patman Act

In the 1920s, the Great Atlantic & Pacific Tea Company (A&P) developed a national chain of grocery stores and began obtaining lower prices than were available to the local grocers.[40] A trade association representing grocery wholesalers sought legislation to prohibit price discrimination in the grocery business. Reflecting equal treatment ideals, Congress decided that banning price discrimination was good for the economy as a whole and enacted the Robinson Patman Act.[41] The Robinson Patman Act bans selling to customers at different prices when the result is likely to substantially harm competition. Because the target of the Act was the

---

[39] Lytle, David B., and Beverly Purdue. "Antitrust Target Area Under Section 4 of the Clayton Act: Determination of Standing in Light of the Alleged Antitrust Violation." Am. UL Rev. 25 (1975).

[40] Levinson, Marc. The great A&P and the struggle for small business in America. Macmillan, 2011.

[41] See *supra* 19.

obtaining of discounts for large quantities by A&P[42], the Act does not allow lower prices for higher quantities unless the lower price is cost justified in an amount equal to the price difference. Meeting, but not beating, a competitive price is a defense to a charge of price discrimination. Courts identified three categories of harm to competition from price discrimination. The first is harm to the competitors of the seller (primary line), the second is harm to the competitors of the favored buyer (secondary line), and the third is harm to the customers of competitors of the favored buyer (tertiary line). When price discrimination was involved, predatory pricing could be alleged as primary line discrimination without the need to show actual or potential monopoly power.

Until about 1980, the Robinson Patman Act was vigorously and strictly enforced by the courts and government enforcers. As a result, most suppliers sold at the same price to all customers, no matter what their size or purchasing capacity was. However, a group of economists known as the 'Chicago School' began asserting in the 1970s that the Robinson Patman Act was actually anticompetitive and should be ignored or substantially limited. Soon after, courts began putting limits on Robinson Patman Act enforcement. First, the sales involved must cross state lines and not merely affect interstate commerce. Second, any damages must be based on lost business and not simply on the fact of a price difference. Third, price differences that are small compared to profit margins are ignored as 'de minimis.' In the last, use against predatory pricing was limited. Action under the Robinson Patman Act are now relatively rare and difficult to win.[43]

---

[42] See *supra* 39.
[43] Hansen, Hugh C. "Robinson-Patman Law: A Review and Analysis." Fordham L. Rev. 51 (1982).

D. The Federal Trade Commission Act

The Justice Department can bring action for criminal violations of the antitrust laws, using grand juries to indict alleged violators, and most antirust criminal actions occurred when the alleged violation was horizontal price fixing. Also, the Justice Department can seek injunctions against threatened violations, such as mergers. However, in civil enforcement, the Justice Department shares responsibility with the Federal Trade Commission.

In 1914, Congress passed the Federal Trade Commission Act, which established the Federal Trade Commission (FTC) with the power to bring civil actions to remedy and punish unfair and deceptive trade practices. Using the power, the FTC can bring actions involving violations of the antitrust laws as well as actions against conduct deemed merely unfair or deceptive. There are no private remedies under the Federal Trade Commission Act.[44]

The Federal Trade Commission Act prohibits unfair methods of competition in interstate commerce, but carries no criminal penalties. It also created the Federal Trade Commission to police violations of the Act.[45]

The Department of Justice also often uses other laws to fight illegal activities, including laws that prohibit false statements to Federal agencies, perjury, obstruction of justice, conspiracies to defraud the United States, and mail and wire fraud. Each of these crimes carries

---

[44] See *generally* Kinter, Earl W., and Christopher Smith. "The Emergence of the Federal Trade Commission as a Formidable Consumer Protection Agency." Mercer L. Rev. 26 (1974).
[45] *Id.*

its own fines and imprisonment terms which may be added to the fines and imprisonment terms for antitrust law violations.[46]

Thus, the commission has enforcement or administrative responsibilities under more than 70 laws, they can be grouped in three categories: 1) Statutes relating to both the competition and consumer protection mission; 2) statutes relating principally to the competition mission; and 3) statutes relating principally to the consumer protection mission. The FTC Act is the primary statute of the Commission. Under this Act, the Commission is empowered, among other things; to 1) prevent unfair methods of competition and unfair or deceptive acts or practices in or affecting commerce; 2) seek monetary redress and other relief of conduct injurious to consumers; 3) prescribe trade regulation rules defining, with specificity, acts or practices that are unfair or deceptive, and establishing requirements designed to prevent such acts or practices; 4) conduct investigations relating to the organization, business, practices, and management of entities engaged in commerce; and 5) make reports and legislative recommendations to Congress.[47]

E. The Enforcement of the Antitrust Laws

There are three main ways in which the Federal antitrust laws are enforced: 1) Criminal and civil enforcement actions brought by the Antitrust Division of the Department of Justice; 2)

---

[46] Averitt, Neil W. "The Meaning of Unfair Methods of Competition in Section 5 of the Federal Trade Commission Act." BcL REv. 21 (1979).
[47] *Id.*

civil enforcement actions brought by the Federal Trade Commission; and 3) lawsuits brought by private parties asserting damage claims.[48]

The Department of Justice uses a number of tools in investigating and prosecuting criminal antitrust violations. Department of Justice attorneys often work with agents of the Federal Bureau of Investigation (FBI) or other investigative agencies to obtain evidence. In some cases, the Department may use court authorized searches of businesses and secret recordings by informants of telephone calls and meetings. The Department may grant immunity from prosecution to individuals or corporations who provide timely information that is needed to prosecute others for antitrust violations, such as bid rigging or price fixing.[49]

A provision in the Clayton Act also permits private parties injured by an antitrust violation to sue in Federal court for three times their actual damages plus court costs and attorneys' fees. State attorney generals may bring civil suits under the Clayton Act on behalf of injured consumers in their States, but groups of consumers often bring suits on their own. Such civil suits, following criminal enforcement actions, can be a very effective additional deterrent to criminal activity.[50]

Most states also have antitrust laws closely paralleling the Federal antitrust laws. The state laws generally apply to violations that occur wholly in one state. These laws typically are enforced through the offices of state attorney generals.[51]

---

[48] Areeda, Phillip, Donald F. Turner, and Herbert Hovenkamp. Antitrust law: an analysis of antitrust principles and their application. Vol. 2. Aspen law & business, 1978.
[49] *Id.*
[50] *Id.*
[51] *Id.*

2. Statutory Structure

A. The Relationship of the Sherman Act to the Common Law

The legislative history of the Sherman Act shows that Congress intended to incorporate and federalize the common law antitrust precedents.[52] However, a problem of interpretation arose, because no unified common law of trade restraints existed. The common law in 1890 included English as well as American judge-made decisions and statutes,[53] espousing the contemporary economic philosophies.[54] As James May explained:

> The congressman who drafted and passed the Sherman Antitrust Law thought they were merely declaring the illegality of offenses that the common law had always prohibited. Like others, they have too easily, accepted the mistaken view that the attitude of the common law towards freedom of trade was essentially the same throughout its history.[55]

The framers of the Sherman Act used terms known in the common law when they condemned monopolies and contracts, combinations, and conspiracies in restraint of trade. In the Senate, where the Act was drafted, most of those who spoke referred to the common law. Senator Sherman himself said that "it does not announce a new principles of the common law."[56] But Senator Sherman's remarks contain some contradictions as to what the common law was and

---

[52] 21 Cong. Rec. 2456, 3146, 3151-52 (1890).

[53] Hans B. *Thorelli, The Federal Antitrust Policy: Origination of an American Tradition* 10 (1954).

[54] *See generally* Herbert Hovenkamp, *The Sherman Act and the Classical Theory of Competition*, 74 Iowa L. Rev. 1019 (1989).

[55] *See generally* James May, *Antitrust Practive and Procedure in the Formative Era: The Constitutional and Conceptual Reach of State Antitrust Law*, 1880-1918, 135 U. Pa. L. Rev. 495 (1987).

[56] 21 Cong. Rec. 2456 (1890).

as to what the bill might do. Senator Hoar, who was closely involved in drafting the final version in the committee, told the Senate that "we have affirmed the old doctrine of the common law" and later said "monopoly is a technical term known to the common law."[57] Senator Edmunds, who was chairman of the Judiciary Committee, spoke to the same effect.[58]

It does not follow that Congress purported to enact the common law. Congress neither specifically adopted any particular English doctrines nor those of any state. Indeed, at the time the Sherman Act was passed the common law was in an unsettled state, and there was little consensus about its meaning. Neither the statute nor its legislative history gives any concrete meaning to "restraint of trade," and the section 2 reference to "monopolize" is even less clear, for the monopoly known to the common law was that granted or held by public or quasi-public authority.[59] Thus, the use of unelaborated common law words and references seems simply to have invested the federal court with a new jurisdiction.[60]

Creation of a new federal jurisdiction inevitably required the courts to receive, apply, and develop "the common law" in the same way that a new jurisdiction customarily does. Perhaps the enactment of the Sherman Act itself could be taken as a legislative indication of the proper direction. The debates do speak of competition, private enterprise, and the control of excess private power. One could marshal examples from the American legal and intellectual tradition of opposition to exclusive privilege or over whelming private power. Certainly, there was many smaller businessmen in 1890 who saw themselves endangered by the trusts and monopolies. Many saw competition as the guardian of equal opportunity and the common right of each

---

[57] 21 Cong. Rec. 3146, 3152 (1890).
[58] *Ibid.*
[59] Herbert Hovenkamp, The aAntitrust Enterprise: Principle and Execution ch.7 (2006).
[60] Robert H. Bork, *Legislative intent and the Policy of the Sherman Act*, 9 J.L. & Econ. 7, 37 (1966).

individual to choose and pursue a calling unmolested by those more successful, more ambitious, or more powerful than they. Competition is often seen as the dispenser of justice to consumer and producer alike. But query the significance of a legislative history so lacking in careful weighing or deliberate choices. Thus, the Sherman Act may be seen not as a prohibition of any specific conduct but as a general authority to do what common law courts usually do.

B. Legislative Landscape and the Dynamics of Clayton Act

The presidential election campaign of 1912 gave considerable emphasis to additional antitrust legislation. To the proponents of additional legislation, the Supreme Court's 1911 interpretation of Sherman Act §1 to forbid only unreasonable restraints of trade[61] portended undue judicial hospitality for anticompetitive conduct. Proposed legislation emerged from the House of Representatives to impose criminal sanctions on certain (1) price discriminations with intent to injure a competitor; (2) exclusive dealing arrangements without significant regard for effects; (3) stock acquisitions substantially lessening or eliminating competition; and (4) refusals to sell oil, coal, or energy. The Senate version eliminated the criminal provisions and left most price discrimination, tying and exclusive dealing matters to the discretionary authority of the new Federal Trade Commission (FTC) to prevent "unfair methods of competition." The Conference Committee compromised these differences by eliminating criminal penalties. The ultimate enactment proscribed certain price discriminations in §2, tying and exclusive dealing arrangements in §3, and mergers by stock acquisition in §7 "where the effect … may be

---

[61] *Standard Oil Co. v. United States,* 221 U.S. 1 (1911).

substantially to lessen competition or tend to create a monopoly in any line of commerce." In addition, §8 prohibited certain interlocking corporate directorates; §10 addressed common carrier transactions, and the remaining sections affected procedures.[62]

The ultimate House-Senate compromise makes it difficult to identify the exact objective of the actual enactment. The Conference Report stated no general rationale.[63] The earlier Committee reports were addressed to bills that were quite different from the ultimate statute. Nevertheless, the following language from the Senate Report resembles what courts have repeatedly said about the purpose of the Clayton Act[64]:

> Broadly stated, the bill, in its treatment of unlawful restraints and monopolies, seeks to prohibit and make unlawful certain trade practices which, as a rule, singly and in themselves, are not covered by the [Sherman Act] … or other existing antitrust acts, and thus, by making these practices illegal, to arrest the creation of trusts, conspiracies, and monopolies in their incipiency and before consummation.[65]

The Clayton Act §2 on price discrimination, §3 on tying and exclusive dealing, and §7 on mergers may be compared with the Sherman Act in several obvious ways.[66] First, violations of both statutes warrant equitable relief and treble damages, but only Sherman Act violations are criminal. Second, unlike the Sherman Act's general prohibitions of trade restraints and monopolization, the Clayton Act is more specific. Third, the Clayton Act's greater specificity is

---

[62] See *supra* 22.
[63] Conference Report, *supra*, S. Doc. No. 585.
[64] Handler, Milton. "Some Misadventures in Antitrust Policymaking. Nineteenth Annual Review." The Yale Law Journal 76.1 (1966): 92-126.
[65] *Id.*
[66] See *supra* 22.

qualified by certain technical limitations not found in the Sherman Act. For example, Clayton Act §§2-3 do not seem to apply to transactions in services or intangibles; they apply only to transactions in tangible goods for sale or use in the united States; and §7, before 1950, covered only stock acquisitions from corporations, not asset acquisitions.[67] Before 1980, §7 covered only acquisitions from corporations, not those from individuals.[68] Fourth, both statutes require various effects as prerequisites to condemnation, although the effects are not defined with much precision. We have already quoted the Clayton Act effects clause and have noted that the Sherman Act §1 is interpreted to condemn only unreasonable restraints of trade. Fifth, although it makes no difference in practice, the Federal Trade Commission, which enforces the Clayton Act directly, enforces the Sherman Act indirectly by incorporating its prohibitions in the FTC Act §5.[69]

Standard of liability under the Sherman and Clayton Acts have in fact coalesced on most matters common to both. First, both are coalesced in terms of the propriety and importance of that development. Some practices are undoubtedly covered by both statutes. For example, a tying agreement compelling the buyer of one product to take tis requirements of a second product from that seller is both a "contract … in restraint of trade" under the Sherman Act §1 and also an "agreement … that the … purchaser … shall not use… the goods … of a competitor … of the … seller" under the Clayton Act §3. The transaction would be unlawful under §1 if "unreasonable" in the particular situation or in general, or unlawful under §3 "where the effect … may be

---

[67] See *supra* 22.

[68] *Id.*

[69] *See* 15 U.S.C. §21, giving the FTC direct authority over provisions of the Clayton Act, limited by the authority of the Surface Transportation Board (formerly the Interstate Commerce Commission), Federal Communications Commission, Department of Transportation, and the Board of Governors of the Federal Reserve System with respect to firms within their jurisdiction (certain common carriers, communications, carriers, air carriers, and banks, respectively).

substantially to lessen competition." Neither standard of illegality has any historical or analytical meaning apart from a determination that the particular restraint or class of restraints excessively burdens competition relative to its procompetitive justifications, if any, and the possible, less restrictive alternatives. And no difference in the criteria for illegality or the mode of analysis follows from the difference between the "unreasonable" formula of the Sherman Act and the "substantial lessening of competition" formula of the Clayton Act. The relevant antitrust policy considerations are independent of the verbal formula used.

C. Legislative Landscape and Dynamics of the Federal Trade Commission Act

The background of the Federal Trade Commission Act and the FTC itself is summarized by Robert Cushman:[70]

The Sherman Antitrust Act of 1890, unlike the Interstate Commerce Act, did not set up an administrative commission to aid its enforcement. It relied for that purpose on the Department of Justice and the courts. The actual enforcement of the act did not inspire public confidence either in the adequacy of the law or in the zeal of the Attorney General in prosecuting those who violated it. A conviction that new and clarifying antitrust legislation was necessary was reinforced by the Supreme Court's announcement of the "rule of reason" in the *Standard Oil* decision of 1911. If the Sherman Act did not prohibit

---

[70] This Paragraph is intended to be no more than a brief introduction to the operations of the FTC and is not intended as a comprehensive guide to practice before that agency. For that purpose one is wise to consult the FTC Operating Manual, the FTC's Web site, http://www.ftc.gov, or other practice materials cited herein. On the legislative history through the eyes of contemporaries, see James A. Emery, A Handbook of The Federal Trade Commission Act: A Review of Its Legislative History and of the Powers, Duties and Procedures of the Commission (1915); Gilbert Holland Montague, *Unfair Methods of Competition*, 25 Yale L.J. 20 (1915).

all restraints of trade, but only those that were unreasonable, then some way ought to be devised to let the businessmen know in advance which was which. Antitrust laws should be enforced not merely by inflicting punishments but through the steady supervision of a permanent administrative agency.[71]

As put by the House managers in the Conference Report:[72]

It is now generally recognized that the only effective means of establishing and maintaining monopoly, where there is no control of a natural resource as of transportation, is the use of unfair competition. The most certain way to stop monopoly at the threshold is to prevent unfair competition. This can be best accomplished through the action of an administrative body of practical men thoroughly informed in regard to business situations, so as to eradicate evils with the least risk of interfering with legitimate business operations.

It is impossible to frame definitions which embrace all unfair practices. There is no limit to human inventiveness in this field . . . . It is also practically impossible to define unfair practices so that the definition will fit business of every sort in every part of this country. Whether competition is unfair or not generally depends upon the surrounding circumstances of

---

[71] *Id.*

[72] Henderson, Gerard Carl. The Federal Trade Commission: A Study in Administrative Law and Procedure. Agathon Press, 1924.

the particular case. What is harmful under certain circumstances may be beneficial under different circumstances.[73]

Perhaps worth noting is Congress' apparent view that a monopoly was not "natural," or prolonged without fault, but that its durability depended on the existence of "unfair," or presumably exclusionary practices. In addition, Congress believed that a Commission of "practical" people who are "informed in regard to business" was somehow better than courts of general jurisdiction for identifying and controlling such practices.

The FTC Act compares with the Sherman and Clayton Acts in the following ways[74]: 1) the scope of the prohibitive powers conferred on the Commission is distinctively worded; 2) its prohibitions are administered by an "agency," which has greater independence from the Executive Branch than the Justice Department is thought to have; 3) that agency makes adjudicatory decisions in the manner of a trial court, and its findings of fact and conclusions of law are reviewed by an appellate court; 4) sanctions are generally equitable in character and prospective in application and not initiated or implemented by private parties; 5) the agency may enter binding consent orders; and 6) it may make more general substantive rules. These points are briefly elaborated.[75]

---

[73] Conference Report, H.R. Rep. No. 1142, 63d Cong., 2d Sess. 18-19 (1914).
[74] Cf. Richard A. Posner, The Federal Trade Commission: A Retrospective, 72 Antitrust L.J. 761, 765 (2005):
The question then is what having an administrative agency, the FTC, adds. There are three possible answers: (1) the FTC has a broader mandate – it can reach practices that while anticompetitive do not amount to full-blown antitrust violations, and it can protect consumers against oppression that might not amount to common law or criminal fraud; (2) as an administrative agency, it has capacities denied to the ordinary courts; and (3) there are benefits to competition among law enforcers.
[75] Id.

There is no private right of action for violations of the Federal Trade Commission Act.[76] The Commission may not issue preliminary orders to preserve the status quo pending the completion of its own proceedings or any appeal from its orders, but a 1973 amendment of the FTC Act authorizes the district courts to grant temporary injunctions upon suit by the Commission at any time before its own order becomes final and even before issuance of its own complaint upon "a proper showing that, weighing the equities and considering the Commission's likelihood of ultimate success, such action would be in the public interest."[77] Unlike a private plaintiff, the FTC need not show irreparable harm,[78] but it must show some chance of ultimate success.[79] Once the court finds such success likely, the court may go so far as to order divestiture of a firm that had already been acquired.[80]

---

[76] *Korzeniowski v. NCO Fin. Sys.*, 2010 WL 466162, 2010-11 Trade Cas. *Accord Jeter v. Credit Bureau, Inc.*, 754 F.2d 907, 912 n.5 (11th Cir.), *on reh'g,* 760 F.2d 1168, 1174 n.5 (11th Cir. 1985); *Holloway v. Bristo-Myers Corp.*, 485 F.2d 986 (D.C. Cir. 1973).

[77] *See* §13(b), 15 U.S.C. §53(b), *applied in FTC v. H.J. Heinz Co.*, 246 F.3d 708, 714 n.5 (D.C. Cir. 2001). The literal language of this provision might suggest that it may be invoked only to prohibit acts that are themselves antitrust violations and not to enjoin conduct that merely impairs the Commission's ability to obtain complete relief through divestiture at a later stage. This question was raised but not resolved in *FTC v. British Oxygen Co.*, 529 F.2d 196, 199 (3d Cir. 1976).
Before 1973, the Commission could seek preliminary relief from an appeals court as an incident to the latter's ultimate power to review FTC orders. FTS v. Dean foods Co., 384 U.S. 597, 605, 611-12 (1966), held that the court of appeals has jurisdiction to issue a preliminary injunction under the All Writs Act, 28 U.S.C. §1651(a) (1964), to prevent consummation of a merger "upon a showing that an effective remedial order, once the merger was implemented, would otherwise be virtually impossible, thus rendering the enforcement of any final decree of divestiture futile"; the court also held that the FTC has standing to seek preliminary relief under those circumstances. The FTC complaint had stated that it was probable that an FTC order would be entered finding a violation of Clayton Act §7.

[78] *FTC v. Whole Foods Mkt., Inc.*, 548 F.3d 1028, 1034-35 (D.C. Cir. 2008); *FTC v. Merchant Servs. Direct*, LLC, 2013 Trade Cas.

[79] *FTC v. Cardinal Health, Inc.*, 12 F. Supp. 2d 34,44 (D.D.C. 1998):
Under section 13(b) of the Federal Trade Commission Act, 15 U.S.C. §53(b), this Court may grant preliminary injunctive relief to the FTC if it finds, upon "weighing the equities and considering the Commission's likelihood of ultimate success," that the injunction would be in the public interest. [Citing *FTC v. Weyerhaeuser Co.*, 665 F.2d 1072, 1074 (D.C. Cir. 1981).] Accordingly, to prevail under Section 13(b), the FTC must demonstrate: (1) a likelihood of success on the merits in its case under Section 7 of the Clayton Act; and (2) that the equities tip in favor of injunctive relief. [Citing *FTC v. Staples, Inc.*, 970 F. Supp. 1066, 1071(D.D.C. 1997)] Where the FTC has not established a likelihood of success on the merits, the Court cannot rely on the equities alone to justify the issuance of a preliminary injunction. [Citing *FTC v. Owens-Illinois, Inc.*, 681 F. Supp. 27, 52 (D.D.C.), *vacated as moot*, 850 F. 2d 694 (D.C. Cir. 1988).]

[80] *FTC v. Elders Grain, Inc.*, 868 F.2d 901, 904-05 (7th Cir. 1989).

The FTC is empowered to issue "cease and desist" orders, which typically carry no criminal or civil penalties for past conduct. However, courts have given the FTC power to recover, or require "disgorgement," wrongfully obtained monopoly profits. However, the main FTC remedies resemble a judicial injunction in that they prevent further unlawful action[81]. The Commission "is the expert body to determine what remedy is necessary to eliminate the unfair or deceptive trade practices which have been disclosed. It has wide latitude for judgement and the courts will not interfere except where the remedy selected has no reasonable relation to the unlawful practices found to exist."[82]

Chapter II. The Movement in American Antitrust Law

1. The Five Stages of Modern Movements

First, the United States Supreme Court's 1977 landmark decision in *Continental T.V., Incorporated v. GTE Sylvania* signaled a new era of antitrust law. The changes in the wake of *Sylvania* have made antitrust law one of the most challenging and exciting fields of contemporary law. At times it is also bewildering. Business activities that were once subject to "bright line" tests of legality are increasingly judged under the elusive "rule of reason" standard. For example, it can no longer be stated with confidence that pricing agreements among

---

[81] Gard, Stephen W. "Purpose and Promise Unfulfilled: A Different View of Private Enforcement Under the Federal Trade Commission Act." Nw. UL Rev. 70 (1975).
[82] *Jacob Siegel Co v. FTC*, 327 U.S. 608, 612-13 (1946).

competitors are *per se* violations of §1 of the Sherman Act. Similarly, mergers that were readily condemned previously are now commonplace. Pervading these changes is an increased reliance by the courts and by the public enforcement agencies on the sophisticated economic analysis. It is clear that the economic approach to antitrust law announced in the *Sylvania* case and the judicial philosophy compatible with that approach remain dominant. Also, the teaching of the *Sylvania* case had influenced the law of both vertical and horizontal restraints.[83]

Second, since the *Sylvania* case had influenced antitrust laws, those teachings have been applied even further afield. The Supreme Court announced though standards for plaintiffs relying on a theory of predatory pricing. Additional hurdles have been erected for private parties attempting to enforce the Robinson-Patman Act. In its latest term, the decisions concerning such threshold issues of summary judgement, antitrust standing, and antitrust injury are also generally consistent with the view that antitrust laws should play a smaller role in modern society. However, antitrust law is nothing if not complex. While its influence may be withering, there continue to be decisions that cannot be easily reconciled with a reduced role. In the past 10 years, the Supreme Court has indicated that there is a lasting and important role for *per se* rules in appropriate cases. It has given new hope to plaintiffs in tying cases. It has narrowed, or at least refined, the antitrust exemption for "the business of insurance." More importantly, the Court has, on more than one occasion, been critical of the use of economic theory in the absence of supporting empirical data.[84]

---

[83] Handler, Milton. "Changing Trends in Antitrust Doctrines: An Unprecedented Supreme Court Term--1977." Columbia Law Review 77.7 (1977).
[84] *Id.*

The third significant era of antitrust law was a period during which antitrust law continued to be shaped by the judicial philosophy found in the *Sylvania* case[85]. This perspective was shown in *State Oil v. Khan*[86], in which the Supreme Court overruled *Albrecht v. Herald Company*[87]. More significantly, the lower court reactions to the two Supreme Court decisions made a more noteworthy movement of antitrust law. Courts have begun applying the teachings of both *Eastman Kodak Company v. Image Technical Services*[88] and *Brooke Group Limited. v. Brown & Williamson Tobacco Company*[89]. Additionally, the 1997 Merger Guidelines also influenced overall antitrust law. In those cases, the theory of market power was considered in a more focused manner as was the continuing efforts by courts to make sense of the complexities of market power analysis. In addition, substantial new treatment of antitrust standing, of domestic and international "commerce" issues, and of conspiracy and its multiple permutations, has been applied.[90]

Fourth, lower courts were still in the process of recognizing the importance of two important shifts in antitrust law. The first was an increased emphasis on economic analysis as signaled by the *Sylvania* case and the second was the application of the doctrine of antitrust standing and antitrust injury to narrow the scope of potential antitrust plaintiffs. Even though antitrust law still has been influenced by those two important shifts, the movement was so significant that it required further refinements with respect to these two critical antitrust concerns. In addition, the intervening years witnessed progress towards a predictable standard for

---

[85] The Sylvania Case: Antitrust Analysis of Non-Price Vertical Restrictions, 78 COLUM. L. REv. 1, 34 (1978).
[86] Messe, Alan J. "Economic Theory Trader Freedom and Consumer Welfare: State Oil Co. v. Khan and the Continuing Incoherence of Antitrust Doctrine." Cornell L. Rev. 84 (1998).
[87] 390 US 145 (1968).
[88] 504 U.S. 451 (1992).
[89] 509 U.S. 209 (1993).
[90] Mueller, Dennis C. "Merger policy in the United States: a reconsideration." Review of Industrial Organization 12.5-6 (1997).

predatory prices, an effort by the Supreme Court to describe what a "quick look" analysis means, and much greater sophistication with respect to the analysis of market power. During this period, as with most areas of law, antitrust law also had new challenges as the world changed. The new challenges stemmed from continued economic globalization and technological advances. Globalization required consideration of the international reach of the United States' antitrust law. Technological change required one to consider the intersection of antitrust law and intellectual property. During that year, the most significant case was the *Microsoft* case and it was implicated for a variety of areas including monopolization, market power analysis, and tying doctrine.

In the most recent period, the United State Supreme Court was in the midst of reshaping antitrust law to reflect its philosophy and to achieve greater consistency. For example, the Court moved resale price maintenance (RPM) from the list of *per se* unlawful activities. To many, this change was a necessary, albeit belated, response to the Court's *Sylvania* decision over 30 years ago. The Court has also made it clear that it would treat secondary line price discrimination, perhaps the last remaining element of the populous antitrust philosophy of the 1960s, in a matter consistent with its emphasis of efficiency. In addition, the Court made one of its first forays into the theory of monopsony and addressed the question of how antitrust law applies to market power on the buying side of the market. In addition, the Court's newly announced position of RPM raises a number of issues. Specifically, many past decisions by the Supreme Court and lower court reflect either approval or disapproval of the *per se* status of RPM. Recently, the rule has been changed and the relevance of that law is in question. Also, a truly consistent antitrust policy required close attention to various exemptions. Exemptions based on non-economic considerations are hard to reconcile with the path the Court has chosen. Moreover, in a global economy, matters of market power and the competitive impact of various agreements must be viewed from an international perspective.[91]

2. Rule Determination

A. The *Per se* Rule

Antitrust law adopts presumptions to cope with an uncertain and untidy reality, and these presumptions may decide what is legally relevant and what inferences may or must be drawn from certain facts or in the absence of other facts. Also, such presumptions are articulated with varying degrees of definiteness and formality. These presumptions, whether the most formal *per se* rules or informal, are rules of substantive law. Moreover, the choice of a rule, whether *per se*, rule of reason, or an intermediate level of inquiry, always presents a question of law. In reality, legal institutions face inevitable uncertainties about the past and future conducts, and fact-finding is extremely costly. Thus, to cope with such uncertainties and expense, the law locates fact-finding in some tribunal and accepts the tribunal's intuitions and judgments, unless they are obviously arbitrary.

The need for presumptions in aid of fact-finding is readily apparent, because these presumptions are conditional on given facts, some are rebuttable with further evidence, and some are actually or virtually irrebuttable. Antitrust law also frequently makes presumptions of a

---

[91] See *generally* Thomas R. *Resale price maintenance: Economic theories and empirical evidence*, (1984).

different kind, and it has characterized much of antitrust law. For example, a court might forbid an inquiry because the government statute expressly precludes it. It is analogous when the courts explain and apply such general statutory standards as "reasonable behavior" or "substantial effect."

The Sherman Act §1 condemnation of every restraint of trade has been understood, at least since 1911, to forbid only "unreasonable" restraints of trade.[92] And various Clayton Act provisions apply only to conduct "where the effect … may be substantially to lessen competition."[93] Furthermore, the Sherman Act §2 proscription of monopolization often depends on a finding that the monopolist's conduct was in some sense unreasonable.[94] The concept of a monopoly itself may depend on a finding that market power is very substantial and persistent. These incomplete statements are meant only to stress that the antitrust statutes, as construed, make legality depend on judgments about reasonableness, substantiality, and similar concepts that are not self-defining.

Under the *Standard Oil* case, the courts saw that certain agreements are intrinsically unreasonable because of "their necessary effect."[95] For example, the typical price-fixing agreement among competitors came to be described as unlawful "*per se*," which literally means "by itself" and which operationally means without regard to proof in the particular case of the collaborators' power, their purpose, or the effects. Consequently, the rule rests on various judgments about facts, economics, and social policy.

---

[92] *Supra* 22.
[93] *Supra* 18.
[94] Pub. L. No. 94-435, Title 3, Sec. 305(a), 90 Stat. 1383 at p. 1397
[95] *Standard Oil, supra*, 221 U.S. at 65.

However, even such strong presumptions as the *per se* illegality can be diverged in two ways. First, for instance, the decision to characterize challenged conduct as "price fixing," "boycotting," or "tying" will often reflect judgments about the legitimacy of the conduct. More specifically, under the *Northwest Wholesale* case, cooperative's enforcement procedures challenged as concerted refusal were "designed to increase economic efficiency and render markets more, rather than less, competitive."[96] This is very sensible because the classification should reflect the applicability to a particular case of the judgments of fact and policy that underlie a *per se* rule. Second, even though the *per se* prohibitions are strong rules the courts also express exceptions. These expressed exceptions help a later court to consider the merits of a new defense. In addition, the later court must be free to consider and allow new defenses notwithstanding earlier uses of the *per se* rule. Thus, a decision that something is unlawful *per se* does not preclude later reexamination and possible alteration of the sweep, application, or character of the rule. However, in the constitutional setting the Supreme Court has indicated that it will overrule earlier decisions only when social facts "or an understanding of facts, changed from those which furnished the claimed justifications for the earlier constitutional resolutions."[97] In antitrust cases, the court has stated the issue rather differently. In *Khan*, the Court concluded that the *per se* rule then applied to maximum resale price maintenance was defensible, if at all, only on grounds of *stare decisis* inadequate to support that rule.[98] Generally, *stare decisis* is weaker when the old rule has ambiguous characteristics and allowed exceptions. Thus, learning that a practice once thought inherently anticompetitive actually has significant beneficial explanations should always invite reconsideration. Under the *Illinois Tool Works* case, the

---

[96] *Northwest Wholesale, supra*, 472 U.S. at 295.
[97] *Planned Parenthood v. Casey*, 505 U.S. 833, 862-63 (1992).
[98] *State Oil Co. v. Khan*, 552 U.S. 3, 20 (1997).

Supreme Court shows that the decision should be overruled by a change of government policy.

The Supreme Court initially accepted the government's argument, made in the 1940s, that

patented tying products should be accorded a presumption of market power. But the government

had later changed its position, and the Supreme Court once again followed the government's

position.[99]

Thus, the illegal *per se* rule has dangerous subset of practice. These are condemned

without an elaborate investigation into market power or the precise reasons for the conduct in the

particular case. A class of conduct is brought within the *per se* rule only after the court has had

sufficient experience with the conduct that it can be fairly certain that the conduct is almost

always anticompetitive and almost never socially beneficial. Thus the *per se* rule is one of

administrative convenience. It permits the court to avoid a long, expensive investigation into a

particular market when such an investigation is unlikely to change the court's initial evaluation.
[100]

B. The Rule of Reason

Generally, the law of monopolization contains two elements: 1) proof of the defendant's

monopoly power; and 2) proof that the defendant engaged in an impermissible exclusionary

practice designed to increase the amount or duration of its monopoly. However, not all

---

[99] *Illinois Tool Works, supra*, 547 U.S. at 38-39, which noted that the Court had first explicitly recognized the presumption in *International Salt Co. v. United States*, 332 U.S. 392 (1947).
[100] HERBERT HOVENKAMP, THE ANTITRUST ENTERPRISE: PRINCIPLE AND EXECUTION, at section 5.6, (2005).

exclusionary conduct warrants condemnation of the monopolist, in fact, some such conduct is efficient and should be encouraged.

Thus, the difficult question is whether there are any general guidelines for determining when the *per se* rule should be applied to a joint activity involving competitors, and when they will be entitled to the rule of reason analysis.

Compare with the *per se* rule, much of antitrust arrangement are analyzed under the rule of reason, which requires: (1) a definition of a relevant market and (2) an assessment of competitive or efficiency effects. Once market power and a facially anticompetitive restraint is found, the plaintiff has made out a *prima facie* case of illegality, but the defendant can rebut this showing by proving a legitimate business justification or efficiency benefit for its conduct. If the defendant succeeds in proving a legitimate business justification or efficiency benefit, the burden shifts back to the plaintiff to show that the same justification or benefit could have been attained by some less restrictive alternative. Since the Supreme Court's decision in *Standard Oil Company v. United States*[101], monopolization cases have been governed by the rule of reason. The purpose of the rule of reason in monopolization cases is to enable the court to distinguish between efficient, or competitive exclusionary conduct, and inefficient, or anticompetitive exclusionary conduct.[102]

However, too sharp a dividing between *per se* rules and the rule of reason would be misleading. The *per se* rule itself reflects past judgments about the factors relevant to the rule of reason, and adoption of a rule of *per se* illegality reflects a prior judicial judgment about the relevant facts and factors bearing on the appraisal of a class of conduct. Moreover, those prior

---

[101] 221 U.S. 1, 31 S.Ct. 502 (1911)
[102] *Id* at 70.

judgments are not ordinarily reopened. But such relatively settled judgments should not, and do not, preclude the courts from thinking afresh about them in connection with issues of classification, new defenses, or general modification.

The absence of *per se* illegality does not necessarily mean that an arrangement warrants deep or extensive inquiry. One can sometimes weigh harms, benefits, and alternatives and conclude almost instantaneously that conduct is either lawful or unlawful. One decides such a case so rapidly that the casual observer might express the result in language of *per se* legality or illegality. Even short of such rapid assessment, the court frequently utilizes decisive presumptions without speaking in *per se* or presumptive terms. Sometimes, courts have used the terms "nearly naked" or "quick look" to capture modes of analysis that seem to be somewhat more elaborate than *per se* examination, but not significantly so.

In terms of presumptions, certain kinds of arrangements are ordinarily held lawful, although the challenger can prevail by a showing of particular facts. For instance, an agreement for the pooling of technology by two small firms in an industry of numerous other firms is almost certain to be lawful. Some conceivable circumstances might dictate a contrary conclusion, but their rarity makes it sensible to see such a pool as presumptively lawful among collaborators who account for a small portion of an industry. Similarly lawful, except in rare circumstances, would be a firm's decision to provide for itself a product or service that it formerly purchased from others[103] or its unilateral decision to restrict the distribution of its product.[104] For a less comprehensive presumption, consider a firm's refusal to sell its product to the plaintiff. There are

---

[103] E.g., *Paschall v. Kansas City Star Co.*, 727 F.2d 692 (8th Cir.),(en banc), *cert. denied*, 469 U.S. 872 (1984)(lawful for dominant newspaper to cease distribution through independent carriers and switch to employee carriers).
[104] E.g., *Continental T.V., Inc. v. GTE Sylvania, Inc.*, 433 U.S. 36 (1977).

circumstance in which refusal to sell might be unlawful, but in the absence of such circumstances, the refusal to deal standing alone must be considered presumptively lawful.[105] Indeed, not even the monopolist has a general duty to deal with competitors, although courts nonetheless find occasional exceptions. Ultimately, many antitrust rules excuse those who lack substantial market power or the means of attaining it.

The value of the *per se* rule rely on its great potential to reduce the costs of litigation. Thus the value of the *per se* rule lost the merit unless pre-trial litigation does not have to address all rule of reason issues. Because, drawing on the relevant market and actual anticompetitive effects are the most costly litigation elements. Therefore, these three factors often operate to undermine the cost savings that *per se* rules make possible: (1) ambiguity about which rule is to be applied; (2) deferral of the proper rule until the judgment stage; and (3) making judgments that are final and with prejudice.

Generally, antitrust law is filled with presumptions. Some are very firm and admit very few exceptions, whereas some allow more exceptions. It is also quite conditional and often is overcome. Some are formally expressed as presumptions. Others are rolling presumptions that dictate the conclusion of fact or law when certain facts are known, but they change or disappear when other facts are known or are replaced by yet other tentative presumptions when additional facts appear. Whether formal or informal, intense or weak, fixed or rolling, such presumptions are the means by which we reach intelligible and consistent conclusions in the uncertain world of antitrust. Through such presumptions, legal institutions cope with our inevitable ignorance about

---

[105] *United States v. Colgate & Co.*, 250 U.S. 300, 307 (1919); *contrast Eastman Kodak Co. v. Image Technical Servs.*, 504 U.S. 451, 479 (1992).

the particular facts of a case, about the general facts of the marketplace, and about the economic

and social significance of one decision or another.

It makes little difference whether we call these presumptions "rule of evidence" or

"substantive rules." We prefer the latter designation, because these presumptions are grounded in

substantive policies of antitrust law relative to one's understanding of the functioning of the

economy. Whatever it is called, it guides the intellectual process of trying to reach intelligent,

disciplined, and consistent conclusions in an untidy universe. They apply uniformly in every case

of a similar kind, and they determine the decisional process of judge sitting without a jury after a

full trial. These presumptions also guide the instructions given to a jury, the allocation of

function between judge and jury, the appropriateness of summary judgment, and, to a lesser

degree, the adequacy of antitrust pleadings.

C. Transition of Court's Application: *Per se* vs. Rule of Reason

So far, the Supreme Court's decision of antitrust cases has developed with several distinct

changes. The two main focuses of the Court are (1) controlling economic concentrations of

industrial power and (2) enhancing efficiency. To overview the Court's changes, I will analyze

the shifting of context of horizontal price-fixing cases.

In *United States v. Trans-Missouri Freight Association*, the Court applied the Sherman

Act section that focuses on the effects of defendants' conduct.[106] The Court said that "worthy

---

[106] 166 U.S. 290 (1897).

man whose lives have been spent in trade or commerce, and who might be unable to readjust themselves to their altered surroundings, mere reduction in the price of the commodity dealt in might be dearly paid for by the ruin of such a class and the absorption of control over one commodity by ab all-powerful combination of capital."[107] In *Chicago Board of Trade v. United States*, the Court put weight on promoting competitive equality rather than economic efficiency.[108] The Court expressed the test of legality as "whether the restrain imposed in such as merely regulates and perhaps thereby promotes competition or whether it is such as may suppress or even destroy competition."[109] This balancing test was too broad to calculate the various competing interests.

In *United States v. Container Corporation*,[110] the Court, especially in Justice Douglas' opinion, rejected the earlier balancing test and focused on the structure of markets as a means to predict market behavior. The Court's reasoning was that the normal market structure will yield competitive environments. Thus the Court avoided balancing social and economic policy concerns.[111] The Court expressed its view that: "The limitation or reduction of price competition brings the case within the ban of § 1 of the Sherman Act, for ... interference with the setting of price by free market forces is unlawful *per se*."[112] The Court applied the illegal *per se* rule rather than rule of reason analysis, because the preserving natural market structure limited the application to balance competing social and economic policy concerns and to economic efficiency arguments.

---

[107] *Id*. at 323.
[108] 246 U.S. 231 (1918).
[109] *Id*. at 238.
[110] 393 U.S. 333 (1969).
[111] For example, in this case, the exchange of current price information among competitors is a violation of the Sherman Act, even when the price exchange yield not higher prices but lower prices. The Court focus on the price stabilizing effect of defendants' conduct, which it resulted from horizontal price exchanges.
[112] *Id*. at 337 (citing *United States v. Socony-Vacuum Oil Co.*, 310 U.S. 150, 224 n.59 (1940)).

However, in *United States v. United States Gypsum Company*, [113] the Court moved from *per se* antitrust analysis to the efficiency-oriented rule of reason analysis. The efficiency analysis derives from the Chicago School's reliance on price theory and its preference for the rule of reason analysis. The rule of reason analysis focuses on competitive harm against economic benefit rather than simply unlawful conduct that directly affects price competition. In addition, the Court applied the rule of reason analysis another cases. For example, in *National Society of professional Engineers v. United States*, [114] the Court express its view regarding the competition effect of the agreements as follows "can only be evaluated by analyzing the facts peculiar to the business, the history of the restraint, and the reasons why it was imposed." [115] Moreover, in *Broadcast Music, Incorporated v. Columbia Broadcasting System, Incorporated* (BMI), [116] the Court also rejected the *per se* illegal analysis as follows "redeeming competitive virtues [of the challenged practice] . . . is not almost sure to be in vain." [117] Those changes of the Court's applications show the future course of Supreme Court antitrust jurisprudence.

Ultimately, on April 2000, the Federal Trade Commission and the Department of Justice announced Guidelines for Collaboration Among Competitors and the Guidelines makes framework regarding to the *per se* and rule of reason analysis.

D. Case Study: Price-Affecting Conduct Case

---

[113] 438 U.S. 422 (1978).
[114] 435 U.S. 679 (1978).
[115] *Id*. at 692.
[116] 441 U.S. 1 (1979).
[117] *Id*. at 13.

In *United States v. Socony-Vacuum Oil Company*, the Supreme Court applied the *per se* rule to an arrangement among major oil producers to allocate gasoline demand. Justice Douglas held that "any combination formed for the purpose and with the effect of raising, depressing, fixed, pegging, or stabilizing the price of a commodity . . . is illegal *per se*."[118]

However, in today, the *Socony-Vacuum* rule must be made subject to at least limited exceptions. For instance, the *Broadcast Music* case[119], certainly delved into Justice Douglas' classification of a *per se* violation, but the Supreme Court applied the rule of reason, even though the application of rule of reason is rare in price-affecting conduct cases.[120]

In the *National Society of Professional Engineers* case[121], the Supreme Court condemned a rule which forbade engineers from bidding competitively for jobs.[122] Their defense was that competitive bidding was not in the public interest, because the result would be that engineers would cut corners and design dangerous structures. The Supreme Court responded by saying that the defense that competition is not in the public interest is inappropriate. In order to receive rule of reason treatment the defendant must show, not that competition in a particular instance is bad, but rather that a particular practice is not anticompetitive. Although the Court did not use *per se* language, its analysis seems most consistent with the *per se* approach.

---

[118] 310 U.S. 150, 60 S.Ct. 811 (1940).
[119] *Accord Broadcast Music, Inc. v. Columbia Broadcasting System, Inc. (BMI)*, 441 U.S. 1, 99 S.Ct. 1551 (1979).
   The Supreme Court approved an arrangement under which thousands of individual artists and other performance right owners licensed their performance rights through "blanket licenses" issued by BMI, which permitted the licenses (mainly radio and television stations) to perform anything in BMI's repertoire. BMI then monitored the licensees to see how often a particular composition was performed, and paid the performance right owners in proportion to the number of uses. (p. 122 BL)
[120] *Id.*
[121] *National Society of Professional Engineers v. United States*, 435 U.S. 679, 98 S.Ct. 1355 (1978).
[122] *Id.*

In addition, in the *Maricopa County Medical Society* case[123], the Supreme Court applied the *per se* rule to an arrangement among doctors and health insurers which fixed maximum prices that the doctors would charge.[124] Under the arrangement, insured patients received a list of participating doctors. If the patient went to a participating doctor, all his costs would be covered by the insurance policy. If he went to a different doctor, he might have to pay the difference between the amounts that doctor charged and the amount covered by the insurance policy. The Supreme Court condemned the arrangement under the *per se* rule, on the theory that maximum price fixing can easily be a cover for minimum price fixing. However, the case has been widely criticized, because the arrangement was nonexclusive and the participation of the health insurers is inconsistent with a doctors' price fixing agreement. Moreover, there was substantial evidence that the arrangement was being used to reduce healthcare costs by facilitating the matching of patients with doctors who agreed not to charge more than a certain amount for their services.

Meanwhile, a price affecting agreement among competitors must generally be public before it will quality for rule of reason treatment. When an arrangement is public from its inception, then the participants have presumably calculated that it does not violate the antitrust laws, probably because it is procompetitive. By contrast, people generally do something in secret because they suspect that what they are doing is wrong and want to avoid detection.

In its decision in the *Indiana Federation of Dentists* case[125], the Supreme Court approved a truncated analysis of a highly suspicious practice, but under circumstances where the Court had only limited experience with the restraint in question. Under this analysis a court may take only a brief look at market power for a restraint that seems highly suspicious, or may dispense with any

---

[123] *Arizona v. Maricopa County Medical Society*, 457 U.S. 332, 102 S.Ct. 2466 (1982).
[124] *Id*.
[125] *FTC v. Indiana Federation of Dentists*, 476 U.S. 447, 106 S.Ct. 2009 (1986).

market power requirement at all, if the defendant cannot offer a reasonable business justification.

Thus, the difference between the "quick look" for highly suspicious restraints and the *per se* rule

that the defendant may be entitled to show either lack of any power to achieve an anticompetitive

result, or an adequate justification. If one of these is found, then the court usually proceeds with

full rule of reason treatment. However, in the *California Dental Associationn* case[126], the

Supreme Court held that the "'quick look' could not be applied to a dental association's rules

that purported to limit deceptive advertising but were in fact so aggressive that they eliminated

nearly all price and quality advertising by dentists."[127] The majority appeared to believe that a

complex market with poorly informed consumers might function as well or better even with

aggressive limitations on advertising.[128] Further, it seemed to think that competitors in such a

market could be trusted to the point that whether such an agreement benefitted consumers or the

providers themselves was a neutral question[129]. As a result, the burden was on the plaintiff to

show that the arrangement had specific anticompetitive outcomes. The four dissenters

emphasized that even in a complex market, truthful claims about price and quality serve to bring

buyers and sellers together, thus enhancing competition. They adhered to the well developed

antitrust rule that when a restraint is highly suspicious and the firms engaged in it have market

power, then anticompetitive consequence can be inferred.[130]

The value of *per se* rule is lost if pre-trial litigation must address all rule of reason. Often

the decision about which rule is to be employed will await facts that are developed only in

discovery. Or the judge might, in appropriate cases, permit a summary judgment motion on a *per*

---

[126] California Dental Assn, v. FTC, 526 U.S. 756, 119 S.Ct. 1604 (1999).
[127] Calkins, Stephen. "California Dental Association: Not a quick look but not the full Monty." Antitrust Law Journal 67.3 (2000).
[128] *Id.*
[129] *Id.*
[130] *Id at 110.*

se record and, if the motion is granted, permit the plaintiff to have further discovery under a rule of reason theory. Such grant would have to be given sparingly, and only to plaintiffs who reasonably but incorrectly believed that the *per se* inquiry should be adequate.

Clearly, the approach must vary with the circumstances, but the basic point should not be lost. Under the current system even a modest chance that the court will apply the rule of reason requires the plaintiff, and thus the defendant, to undergo all the costs of rule of reason preparation. In that case, the resource savings that the *per se* rule promises are largely illusory.

In *Illinois Tool Works*[131], the plaintiff challenged a tying arrangement and rested its proof of power entirely on the fact that the tying product was patented. The plaintiff relied on the Supreme Court's then existing "*per se*" presumption that a tying patented product conferred sufficient power to make the tie unlawful without additional inquiry into market power. The Supreme Court then reversed and rejected the presumption that the Supreme Court had repeatedly recognized[132]:

> The respondent reasonably relied on our prior opinions in moving for summary judgment without offering evidence defining the relevant market or proving that petitioners possess power within it. When the case returns to the District Court, respondent should therefore be given a fair opportunity to develop and introduce evidence on that issue, as well as any other issues that are relevant to its remaining §1 claims.[133]

---

[131] 547 U.S. at 46.
[132] See Illinois Tool Works, Inc. v. Independent Ink, Inc., 547 U.S. 28 (2006). The presumption was created in International Salt Co. v. United States, 332 U.S. 392 (1947), and recognized and expanded to copyrights in United State Wright, Joshua. "Illinois Tool Works v. Independent Ink." Antitrust Chronicle 1 (2007). s v. Loew's Inc., 371 U.S. 38 (1962).
[133] *Id* at 115.

This situation involved an explicit change of law rather than a reasonable, but incorrect prediction, concerning which rule a court would apply. But the difference is readily exaggerated. In this case, the presumption had been badly battered and qualified, and a plaintiff's reliance on it was very likely no more reasonable than reliance on other indicators of *per se* illegality. Indeed, the outcome can produce the result that when the Supreme Court explicitly overrules an earlier decision, the plaintiff gets a second chance, but if the court merely qualifies earlier statements that stated the reach of the *per se* rule broadly, the plaintiff will be held to have selected the wrong rule and will suffer dismissal. Acting *ex ante*, the plaintiff has no choice but to plead and prove a full rule of reason case, and in the process forced the defendant to defend against it. In that case the saving produced by a *per se* rule become imaginary.

Chapter III. Economic Analysis of Antitrust Law

1. Economic Application in Monopoly

The common law has a number of principles protecting the ideas of free enterprise. For example, "restraints on alienation" of real property are against public policy and therefore held void. Also, non-compete agreements between employer and employees are disfavored and must be held "reasonable" in geographic and temporal scope.

In the economist's ideal world of perfect competition, no seller can affect the price or output of a given product and competition produces prices as low as possible and quality as high as possible. If one seller raises its price just a little, buyers can turn to the other sellers, who have the ability to sell the required amount.

The ability of a single firm to deliberately affect the price or supply of an item, is called its market power. In many real cases, individual sellers have a degree of market power because of their size, the uniqueness of their products and/or customer loyalty. Generally, the more market power possessed by the firms in a market, the more likely that prices will be higher than those produced by perfect competition. Market power cannot be measured in the abstract, but must be examined in the context of a relevant market.

The relevant market is the scope of commerce in which meaningful competition takes place and must be defined in terms of both product and geography. Determining market power therefore requires determining both the relevant product market and the relevant geographic market. The relevant geographic market is the geographic area in which competitors face each other in realistic competition. Therefore, market size depends on the relationship between price and transportation costs.

The relevant product market includes those products or services that consumers view as interchangeable when prices increase. If consumers will turn to margarine when the price of butter increases and vice versa, both products will be in the same product market. A product market can also be based on a supplier's ability to produce a different product easily.

Determining the product market often requires elaborate cross elasticity studies, to determine which products are held "interchangeable" by consumers. However, it is generally the case that a relevant product market includes more than the products of a single manufacturer no matter how much brand loyalty that manufacturer may command. Numerous courts have held that all automobiles are in the same product market because they accomplish the same purpose.

However, a single brand may create a relevant product market if a firm creates circumstances that compel consumers to buy from them, as they may be in the case when obtaining replacement parts. The extent of a firm's market power is typically measured by determining its market share in the relevant market. Market shares of 70 percent are usually thought sufficient to create monopoly power. A market share lower than 20 percent or so is usually not considered to create significant market power.

In practice, what a particular market share indicates about market power is affected by market concentration. The fewer firms in a relevant market, the more concentrated that market is. The Herfindahl-Hirschman Index (HHI) is a measure of market concentration. The HHI is determined by adding the squares of the market shares of the top fifty companies in a relevant market. HHI below 1000 indicate that a market is not concentrated and while indexes above 2500 indicate that a market is highly concentrated. A market share analysis may not be the end of the search for market power because current market share reflects only the past and not the future. The market share may not be sustainable, such as a company whose mineral reserves will not last.[134]

2.   Monopolization under the Sherman Act Section 2

Monopoly power is the ability of a single firm to control price entirely on its own and to raise prices without losing business to others. Thus, in general firms with monopoly power can

---

[134] Rhoades, Stephen A. "The herfindahl-hirschman index." Fed. Res. Bull. 79 (1993).

increase their profits by selling at prices significantly higher than the competitive price even though they may lose sales in the process. As a result, firms with monopoly power are seen as allocating resources in an inefficient manner and harming consumer welfare. This is especially true since when fixed costs are a high percentage of total costs, a market may allow only one firm to be profitable. Electric and gas utilities, and some newspapers are therefore considered to be natural monopolies. Natural monopolies are typically regulated to prevent the charging of monopoly prices while still allowing a profitable operation.

Section 2 of the Sherman Act proscribes three separate offenses: monopolization, attempted monopolization, and conspiracy toward monopolization. All offenses now require a relevant market, but Section 2 was originally directed against the monopolies that were seen as destroying small business in the late 19th century.

Even 120 years later, the exact scope of Section 2 remains subject to debate. In a 1945 opinion resolving an action under Section 2 alleging illegal monopolization by Alcoa, which controlled most of the aluminum market, Judge Learned Hand wrote that "the successful competitor, having been urged to compete, must not be turned upon when he wins." Since Section 1 encourages vigorous competition, he questioned whether a company that wins the competitive battle and obtains monopoly power should be punished.

Judge Hand's Comments reflected the uncertainty over exactly what Congress meant by making it illegal to monopolize. The word monopolize can mean either the status of having monopoly power or the conduct involved in obtaining such power. The semantic question of whether "monopolization" is a status offense or a conduct offense or perhaps both, remains unresolved. By ordering the breakup of Aloca, Judge Hand held that only monopoly power thrust upon its holder is exempt from punishment. Since Aloca had expanded its business to keep up with customer demand, its continued monopoly power was the result of its conscious decisions to maintain that power and met the definition of monopolizing. His view prevailed for at least a generation.

In the 1970s, commentators began saying that it is a mistake to interpret Section 2 as directed at lawfully obtained monopolies. Commentators have claimed that that most attempted exercises of monopoly power through high prices will lead others to enter the market, thereby eliminating the monopoly power. These commentators saw lawfully obtained monopoly power as self-correcting and believed that efforts to punish monopoly power are as likely to deter competitive behavior as to protect it.

The above opinion assumes the absence of barriers to entry which inhibit the entrance of new firms to the market. If barriers to entry exist then the high prices created by the exercise of monopolistic power might be insufficient to attract new firms to the market. Barriers to entry include such things as the cost of duplicating facilities and brand loyalty. One of the most significant barriers to entry is government regulation. Examples of such barriers include such regulations as licensing requirements and zoning. When such regulation exists, there is often a need to ensure that even lawfully obtained monopoly power is not extended or abused.

3. Current Views on Monopolization

Although the exact contours of illegal monopolization remain somewhat uncertain, the term clearly encompasses two separate offenses. One offense is the use of lawfully obtained monopoly power to inhibit competition, most clearly in other markets. The other offense is obtaining monopoly power through unreasonably exclusionary or predatory acts. Today, it is reasonably clear that illegal monopolization does not reach businesses that have simply obtained monopoly power by obtaining business from others. A firm with lawfully obtained monopoly power does not use that power simply by charging monopoly price to customers. However, if a firm uses its monopoly power, including its pricing power, to obtain additional market power that use can be illegal. The use of monopoly power is most clearly illegal when it enables the monopolist to obtain power in another relevant market, a tactic called leverage.

The use of leverage was first identified in cases in which the owner of a patented machine required users also to purchase unpatented supplies for that machine. This requirement effectively extended the market power in the patent into the market for supplies, foreclosing competition.

Common leveraging tactics include "tying arrangements" and "refusals to deal." Tying arrangements occur when a company with monopoly power in one product, legal or otherwise, requires customers wanting that product to also buy another product in a different product market. The restriction on choice forces customers to buy the second product at a higher-than-competitive price.

By restricting consumer choice, tying harms both the customer, who is forced to pay high prices for a product due to an artificial restriction on purchasing options, and also harms would-be competitors who lose potential customers. Therefore, tying can be illegal monopolization because it interferes with markets and harms the public.

The "refusal to deal," is the other archetypal leverage tactic. Ordinarily, a company does not have an obligation to sell to anyone and can pick and choose its customers on any basis.

However, a company with monopoly power over a product which is needed in a second market may have an obligation to sell to all customers needing the product to compete in the second market. This is especially true if the monopolist competes in the second market. Refusing to sell the needed product crosses a legally significant line because it, "leverages" power into the second product market.

Terminal Railroad case[135] clearly defines one form of impermissible refusal to sell in terms of the "essential facilities doctrine." The doctrine originated in a Section 1 case in which a group of railroads refused to let a competing railroad use an essential bridge. The elements of an essential facilities claim are 1) control by a monopolist of a facility essential to competition in another market, 2) inability of a competitor in that second market to duplicate the facility, and 3) denial of use of the facility to the competitor.[136]

After the enactment of the Sherman Act, low pricing by a dominant company was attacked as illegal monopolization. The lower prices were seen as a use of monopoly power, the idea being that the low prices were being subsidized by monopoly profits. The validity of this view was particularly easy to observe if the prices were lowered only in certain areas, with prices higher in other areas.

Prior to 1975, determining whether pricing was predatory was a matter of determining the seller's intent. The centrality of intent resulted in monopoly cases hinging on the result of a largely subjective inquiry. If a court determined that pricing was directed at eliminating a

---

[135] 224 US 383 (1912).
[136] Maurer, Stephen M., and Suzanne Scotchmer. "The Essential Facilities Doctrine: The Lost Message of Terminal Railroad." (2014).

competitor, the price was considered to be predatory. If a court determined that the pricing was an effort to obtain additional business, the pricing was seen as legitimately competitive.

In 1975, a law review article by professors Areeda and Turner suggested that the intent test was flawed and was itself anti-competitive[137]. They noted that every competitor wants to increase its business at the expense of its competitors and that such intent is at the heart of competition and should not be punished. They also noted that the elimination of inefficient companies that could not compete with more efficient companies selling above their costs should actually be encouraged.[138]

The Areeda/Turner article suggested that predatory pricing should be found only if the prices are below average variable costs, costs that vary with the amount produced. The idea behind employing this standard was that any price above average variable costs benefits the seller. On the other hand, there is no benefit to selling below variable costs except to destroy competitors because every sale loses money and more money is lost by increasing sales.[139]

The above definition of predatory pricing, with its objective standard based on average variable costs, was almost immediately adopted by the courts. The courts saw embraced the more objective standard, as a way to prevent companies from using antitrust laws to interfere with their more efficient competitors.

In so doing courts made a clear statement that the goal of antitrust laws to protect competition, not competitors. With this evolution of anti-trust theory, companies going out of

---

[137] Areeda, Phillip, and Donald F. Turner. "Predatory pricing and related practices under Section 2 of the Sherman Act." Harvard Law Review (1975).
[138] *Id.*
[139] *Id.*

business as a result of vigorous competition became acceptable, and it now difficult for companies to establish predatory pricing under any legal theory.

Interestingly, the establishment of an objective definition of predatory pricing, inspired some courts to articulate objective differences between competition on the merits[140] and predation[141]. For instance, selling below average variable costs, bringing an expensive lawsuit with no chance of prevailing, adding unnecessary features to products which have no value to consumers but which preclude compatibility with competing products, and refusing to sell a product which is not in short supply to a qualified buyer are the examples of predation.

It is possible at least to sate one difference between monopoly power and illegal monopolization subject to Section 2 with the aid of an objective definition of predatory conduct: A lawful monopoly is one that came into existence through competition on the merits, and unlawful monopoly is one created by the use of predatory or exclusionary acts. Thus, a lawfully obtained monopoly becomes illegal when the power is used in a predatory way or used to obtain leverage in other markets.

Despite the efforts to find objective definitions of predatory conduct, the exact boundary between such conduct and competition on the merits is sometimes less than clear. Courts still look at motives and timing in determining predatory conduct. If certain conduct occurs in response to a new entrant and ceases when the entrant leaves, it is much more likely to be seen as predatory or unreasonably exclusionary.

---

[140] Competition on the merits is conduct that gets its justification from increasing profits or reducing losses regardless of its effect on competition.
[141] Predation is conduct that depends for its justification on competition being destroyed and prices raised to monopoly levels

4.   Attempted Monopolization

Using definitions of attempts from the criminal law, courts have defined the offense of attempted monopolization as including the following three elements; 1) a specific intent to obtain monopoly power, 2) an exclusionary act or predatory act directed toward obtaining such power, 3) a dangerous probability of obtaining monopoly power. Also, like other claims under Section 2, attempted monopolization requires a relevant market.

As one of the three elements, the specific intent required for attempted monopolization is the intent that the acts undertaken will result in the power to increase prices to monopoly levels. In an attempt case based on predatory pricing, it may be necessary to show that the low prices were done with the expectation that any losses could be recouped in the future through higher prices. In some cases, this intent can be inferred from the acts themselves.

Furthermore, in recent cases the acts most likely to be deemed exclusionary or predatory for purposes of attempted monopolization are those that would make a monopoly illegal if it were achieved through those acts. Therefore, an attempt to monopolize is often seen as an unsuccessful effort to obtain a monopoly that would be illegal if monopoly power were obtained. However, courts tend to require more egregious actions in an attempt claim.

Finally, the "dangerous probability" element of attempted monopolization is best understood as a significant likelihood that the acts could eventually lead to the achievement of monopoly power if they were allowed to continue unimpeded. Courts may deem it sufficient that the accused party already has significant market power, typically at least 30 percent market share, without worrying about how much power it might ultimately obtain through the acts in question.

Interestingly, monopolization offenses involving the use of monopoly power can often also be seen as attempted monopolization, especially when leveraging is involved. For instance, tying a monopoly product and a competitive product can be seen both as monopolizing the tying product market by using monopoly power and as attempting to monopolize the tied product market. In either case, courts may require evidence of market power in the second market. Additionally, even (though) Section 1 does not reach unsuccessful efforts to obtain an illegal agreement, if the objective of the illegal agreement is the obtaining of monopoly power in a relevant market, an unsuccessful solicitation of a conspiracy can be attacked as attempted monopolization.

Under an attempted monopolization theory, a relevant market must be established even if a successful conspiracy would have been illegal per se. An "illegal conspiracy to monopolize" requires an agreement between two independent entitles to obtain monopoly power in a relevant market, coupled with an overt act directed toward accomplishing that intent. There is no requirement that the conspiracy have any degree of success. However, since a conspiracy to monopolize claim is usually more difficult to prove than a Section 1 claim, it is rarely asserted as a stand-alone claim.

Chapter VI. The Implication of Substantial Economic Theories in Antitrust Law

1. The Genesis of the Antitrust Debates: Jefferson v. Hamilton.

Based on the writings of Adam Smith and others, one of the guiding principles of the American economy is "free enterprise." The assumption underlying free enterprise is that a plurality of independent actors, each attempting to maximize its own economic welfare, will lead to the lowest prices, the highest quality and the most efficient allocation of society's resources.

Adam Smith's "invisible hand" is a metaphor for the efficiency of free enterprise. In a free enterprise economy, restrictions on the ability of independent actors to make their own economic decisions are seen as creating inefficiencies and dislocations. If two companies agree to "fix" the prices of their products at levels above those established by competition, fewer products will be produced and the prices will be higher. In a free enterprise system, unrestricted competition is the ideal and deviations from the ideal are discouraged.

Free competition is often tough on competitors and competition often produces losers. One of the benefits of competition is that it eliminates the most inefficient market participants, a fact not appreciated by the losers. Furthermore, the pressure of competition produces a tendency for competitors to try to avoid the rigors of competition in order to survive. That fact has been recognized since the days of Adam Smith.

The genesis of the antitrust debate predates the first antitrust statute, the Sherman Act of 1890. The debate is as old as Jefferson and Hamilton's contrasting views on governance.[142] Jefferson advocated a decentralized society and government, one that valued independent decision-making and equality-enhancing opportunities for small, local businesses. Control of

---

[142] See *generally* A.D. Neal & D.G. Goyder, *The Antitrust Laws of the U.S.A.* 439-43, 470 (3d ed. 1980).

economic concentrations of industrial power was central to Jeffersonian populism. Hamilton, on the other hand, feared that decentralization might interfere with the goal of efficiency. He was an exponent of a strong national government, particularly central control over financial and economic issues and institutions.[143] These tension between these contrasting concerns persists in the current field of economics.

Jeffersonianism was evident in the legislative history of the Sherman Act. The Congress that passed the Sherman Act was concerned by business concentration, and feared that acquisition of monopoly power, and the formation of cartels might lead to exploitatively high prices for customers. Additionally, the legislative debate shows that those favoring the legislation repeatedly referenced Jeffersonian themes. For example the importance of entrepreneurial independence, the value of independent decision-making, and of freedom of contracting to a healthy market were all referenced during the debate.

Dispersing economic power and stimulating access to free markets also were principle goals of the legislation. Distributional effects and equity concerns were directed toward protecting consumers from a redistribution of wealth from consumers to monopolists and toward protecting competitors from predatory practices.[144] Generally speaking, these goals are unrelated to the Hamiltonian goal of efficiency.

Hamiltonianism was also evident in the legislative history of the Sherman Act. Rejecting this politically-centered, distributive-goal analysis, some scholars have concluded that the main, if not the sole, purpose behind the Sherman Act was the promotion of economic efficiency.[145]

---

[143] *The Federalist* Nos. 9, 11, 16 (Alexander Hamilton) (Clinton Rossiter ed., 1961).
[144] S. 1, 51st Cong. (1st Sess. 1889), *reprinted in 1 The Legislative History of the Federal Antitrust Law and Related Statutes 89* (Earl W. Kintner ed., 1978); 21 Cong. Rec. 2460, 2457, 3146, 3152 (1890).
[145] Richard A. Posner, *Economic Analysis of Law* 10 (2d ed. 1977); Richard A. Posner, *Antitrust Law: An Economic Perspective* 4, ch. 2 (1976).

Grounded in a more Hamiltonian approach, this theory argues that antitrust policy should sanction business conduct that promotes efficient allocations of resources. For many students of antitrust the ultimate question is whether the challenged practice produces a net gain or loss to the consumer. The resolution of the underlying policy rationale for antitrust is crucial to a contemporary study of antitrust.

Today, there is agreement that the antitrust laws were written primarily to encourage competition.[146] However, the continuing debate over whether the goal of promoting competition was rooted in concern over allocative efficiency or distribution of wealth is not likely to be resolved soon. For instance, the main purpose of the Robinson-Patman Act in 1936 was the protection of small business from the leveraged buying practices of larger business. The same is true for the Clayton Act in 1914, particularly with regard to the 1950 Celler-Kefauver Amendments.[147] The same concerns motivated the Federal Trade Commission Act in 1914 which also had efficiency, and wealth distribution, concerns.

The FTC Act expressed that "Monopoly is the evil we wish to control. Competition is the thing we wish to maintain."[148] Again, monopoly profits are condemned either because they are achieved through allocative inefficiency or because they redistribute income and wealth from consumers to producers. Thus, the issues are how competition is best achieved and what groups in society should benefit from this goal.

---

[146] Robert H. Lande, *Wealth Transfers as the Original and Primary Concern of Antitrust: The Efficiency Interpretation Challenged*, 34 Hastings L.J. 65, 68-70 (1982).
[147] See Derek C. Bok, *Section 7 of the Clayton Act and the Merging of Law and Economics*, 74 Harv. L. Rev. 226, 233 (1960).
[148] 51 Cong. Rec. 8855 (1914) (statement of Rep. Morgan).

2. Economic Implications in the Early Stages

Economic theory has become increasingly important in shaping antitrust law and policy. However, economists originally shunned or were indifferent towards antitrust development, and they did not play a central role in the legislative debates of the Sherman Act. For instance, up to World War I, economists played virtually no role in shaping antitrust policy. The main reason for this was a paucity of empirical studies upon which to base policy judgment. The appearance of a number of industry and firm studies filled this gap. Additionally, the development of "economic realism" in the1930's strengthened the connection between economic theory and antitrust policy[149].

In separate works, Joan Robinson[150] and Edward Chamberlin[151] ushered in economic realism by focusing on market conditions on a continuum between the poles of pure competition and pure monopoly. They noted that in the real world, most industries are imperfectly competitive, with the firms possessing varying degrees of market power.

One of the most important characteristics of imperfect or monopolistic competition is that the fewer the firms competing in a market, the greater the tendency for mutually interdependent conduct.

Another important contribution came from Berle and Means who attacked the notion that ownership and control of enterprise property resided in a single owner-manager who, guided by

---

149 Bourdieu, Pierre. "A reasoned utopia and economic fatalism." New Left Review 227 (1998).
150 J. Robinson, *The Economics of Imperfect Competition* (1933).
151 E. Chamberlin, *The Theory of Monopolistic Competition* (1933).

the "invisible hand," used resources to maximize profits.[152] As a result, management is no longer addicted to profit maximization but is instead free to seek other goals not necessarily in harmony with the competitive system.

Even economic facts began to appear in lawyer's briefs, the emphasis continued to be on abuse and predatory conduct as the determinants of illegality. The situation was such that in a 1937 law review article, economist Edward Mason observed that lawyers and economists are "ceasing to talk the same language."[153] He gave four reasons: (1) confronted with a statute that imposes the concept of public interest, the courts were more likely to focus on conduct imposing direct, rather than direct, injury to enterprise; (2) it was much easier to develop proscriptive standards based upon restrictive conduct; (3) at an earlier period predatory tactics probably did in fact contribute to the monopoly problem; (4) before the Sherman Act, most monopoly actions had been private, and had reflected efforts to redress the damage from predatory conduct.

3. Posner's Theory of the Economic Implications of Antitrust Law

Most scholars agree with that Law and Economic originated from Coase and Calabressi. In addition, there is no dispute that Judge Posner elicited reverberations in the field of economic applications of law by jurists.

The conservative theory in the relationship between law and economics tends to make cost and benefit arguments in support of legal rules that they find to be efficient and against legal

---

[152] A. Berle, G. Means, *The Modern Corporation and Private Property* (1932).
[153] Mason, "Monopoly in Law and Economics," 47 Yale L.J. 34 (1937).

rules that they find to be inefficient. In borrowing heavily from the science of economics, the conservative legal economist tends to imply that the results of their calculations are scientific and seemingly "neutral" and "objective" and free of overt subjective morality. Thus, the conservative legal economists tend to rely on one version or another of the neoclassical model of economics, consequently their analysis is biased by the subjective assumptions of that model.

A. Neoclassical Economic Approaches

By using neoclassical economics, the conservatives reduce the rights and obligations to numerical calculations and then proceed to balance countervailing claims by means of scientific questions. It is argued that an efficient result will maximize wealth and that wealth maximization produces the best attainable social arrangement. Within the conservative vision of law and economics there is no concept of inherent rights of the individual merely as a result of being a human being. Natural rights or inalienable rights are non-existent to the extent that they cannot be factored into the cost-benefit analysis. The most prominent conservative, Judge Richard Posner, in his book "The Economics of Justice," says:

Another implication of the wealth-maximization approach, however, is that people who lack sufficient earning power to support even a minimum decent standard of living are entitled to no say in the allocation of resources unless they are part of the utility function of someone who has wealth. This conclusion may seem to weigh too heavily the individual's particular endowment of capacities. If he happens to be born feeble-minded and his net social product is negative, he would have no right to the means of support even though there was nothing blameworthy in his inability to support himself.[154]

B. Posner's efficiency

As Posner analyzes the law by economic application, his main proposition is that the law should be efficient. That means when reviewing rules and legal principles, economic efficiency can be a standard and measuring tool. Traditionally, the jurists pursue a just decision rather than an efficient decision, because traditionally it is believed that the efficient decision conflicted with the just decision. Thus jurists raise the question that "the efficiency can be a reviewing standard of law." This kind of question links with the question "what is the efficient?" Thus, the efficient decision should be defined first, then we can move to the other question regarding efficiency as the standard of law.

Generally, efficiency can be defined by three methods, such as Pareto, Kaldo-Hicks, and Posner's definition of efficiency. When Pareto and Kaldo-Hicks define efficiency from the utility side, Posner defines efficiency as the concept of maximization of wealth that is measured by willingness to pay. Through this approach, Posner can avoid the criticism of utilitarianism. Under Posner's definition of efficiency, efficiency can be reached at the maximization of wealth. Wealth here does not mean profits and incomes. Economists generally express wealth as a utility, benefit, or welfare. It does not mean a subjective meaning of happiness as a utilitarian idea.

---

[154] R. Posner, *The Economics of Justice* 76 (1983).

Also, Posner's idea of maximizing wealth can be measured by the willingness to pay. Willingness to pay is the maximum amount of money that a person can be paid to acquire something he desires to get. People normally would not pay more than the utility he can get from the purchased item, thus willingness to pay is expressed by the amount of utility. In addition, one's willingness to pay can be compared with others, because the willingness to pay can be measured by a monetary unit.

A monopoly is the representative example to show Posner's efficiency idea. That is, measuring maximize wealth by willingness to pay is the appropriate method of measurement. In addition it can be appropriate as a moral standard. A monopoly market has less output and a higher price than a competitive market. It can result in decreasing customer surplus and increasing the corporate profits. If the decreasing amount of customer surplus is bigger than the increasing amount of corporation profits, then the social welfare will be decreased. The decreasing of social welfare brings inefficiency in its result. If we do not consider the inefficiency part of the monopoly, ethical problems would not come up in monopoly matters.

Posner's suggestion of efficiency can be connected with Pareto efficiency through the Coase theorem. It can be expressed with the following graph. As a famous example of a cattle raiser and a farmer, when the cattle raiser increases the number of cattle, the profit of cattle raiser will be increased but the marginal revenue will also be increased. In addition, the marginal cost of the cattle raiser and the marginal harm of the farmer will be increased. On the graph, the cattle raiser will get the maximum profit when he raises 100 cattle, but Pareto efficiency can be achieved when he raises 50 cattle as both the farmer and the cattle raiser obtain wealth maximization.

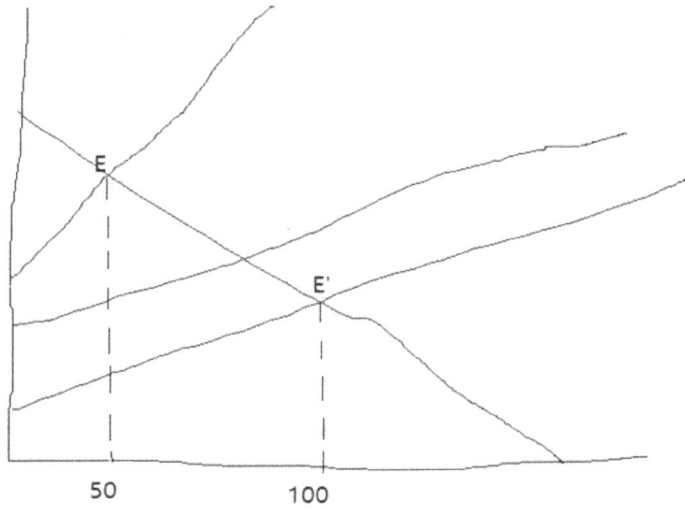

50   100

Under the Coase theorem, if the farmer has an entitlement, the cattle raiser can increase the cattle from 0 to 50 through the negotiation with the farmer. The cattle raiser can get a positive profit even though he has to payoff the farmer's damage, because the cattle raiser's profit (earning- cost) is bigger than farmer's marginal damage until he reaches 50 cattle. Thus, Pareto improvement continues until the cattle raiser increases the cattle until it reaches 50 cattle. However, if the cattle raiser increase cattle to more than 50, the cattle raiser's marginal profit is less than the farmer's marginal damages, thus Pareto improvement is not available. Therefore, 50 cattle is the Pareto optimality.

4. Real Market Application of the Economic Theories

In the economist's ideal world of "perfect competition," no seller can affect the price or output of that product and competition produces prices as low as possible and quality as high as possible. However, the real world is not working like an economist's ideal world. In spite of some imperfections, economists increasingly join the debate as to the economic implications of antitrust. Now, courts routinely use concepts and theories developed by economists and weave economic concepts into decisions to support their results. The premise of antitrust is that some industries contribute best to overall social welfare if they are competitive.[155] Although, it is far from clear as a matter of economics theory that increasing the competitiveness of a particular industry, in the context of other industries that remain highly concentrated, actually increases overall welfare. In a competitive market, consumers attempt to maximize their satisfaction by allocating expenditures among various goods and services. Producers, on the other hand, must direct resources into goods and services that consumers value the most and produce these products at the lowest per unit cost. Thus, the economic theory underlying antitrust centers on price theory or microeconomics, such as the study of individual markets, include how prices and quantities are determined and how products and resources are allocated. In addition to the price theory and microeconomics, in a market driven economic system analyzing individual economic behavior is also important, because the market is controlled by individual decisions. In order to analyze and predict market behavior, economists generalize about individual economic behavior for two basic assumptions: 1) the individual makes market decisions based upon self-interest, such as one buys and sells to maximize one's own personal wealth, utility, or satisfaction; and 2) the aggregates of these individual decisions serve to maximize the wealth of society. Even the

---

[155] See F.M. Scherer, *Industrial Market Structure and Economic Performance* 24-29 (2d ed. 1980).

predictions of the economist are not as reliable as the "truths" produced in the natural sciences. Nevertheless, they do provide a statement of economic tendency, constituting what Boulding labels a "map of reality."[156]

The modern antitrust laws are statutes that were originally proposed during the negotiations preceding the adoption of the General Agreement on Tariffs and Trade (GATT) in 1974, but could not be resolved until the World Trade Organization was created in 1994[157]. The goal of antitrust laws is promoting free and unrestrained competition among business in order to assure the lowest price and highest quality to consumers seemed clear. The antitrust statutes themselves are short and written in cryptic language that has required a great amount of interpretation by courts, and this interpretation has been affected by political and economic considerations. The judgments in this area need to decide between giving preference to intellectual property rights or towards promoting competitiveness.

A. Economic analysis for market power in monopoly

As I discussed before, the question of market power is pervasive in antitrust, and one of the most common cases is from the analysis of agreements between and among firms under Section 2 of the Sherman Act in monopolization and an attempt to monopolize cases.

A firm's market power can be measured by the Lerner Index which is expressed mathematically as follows:

---

[156] K. Boulding, *Economic Analysis* 15 (1941).
[157] See The *Agreement Establishing the WTO* included a range of limited provisions on various cross-border competition issues on a sector specific basis.

$$L = (P-C)/P$$

L is the Lerner Index, P is the firm's profit maximizing price and C is the marginal cost at the profit maximizing output.[158] Since the price charged under competitive conditions is equal to marginal cost, the formula measures the difference between the firm's profit maximizing price and the competitive price divided by the profit maximizing price.[159] The higher the index the greater the firm's market power. Of course, a firm's ability to charge a price above competitive levels is related to the elasticity of demand it faces. Thus, the Lerner Index is equal to the reciprocal of the elasticity of the firm's demand curve, or mathematically $1/Ed$.[160] Therefore, a lower elasticity means a higher index and greater market power, and a higher elasticity means a lower index and less market power. However, the Lerner Index often only provides a theoretical sense, since the data required to make the actual calculation are often unavailable. Thus, courts have traditionally started from the premise that market share- the firm's sales in the market divided by total sales- is typically used as a proxy for market power.[161]

As a measure of market power, market share data alone may be unreliable because it is only one of the determinant powers, and the determination of market share required defining the relevant product and geographic market that are far from an exacting process. Additionally, the standard view in antitrust is that a high market share, without more, is something to be avoided. In recent years, particularly in the wake of *United States V. Microsoft Corp.*,[162] the problem of

---

[158] The discussion of the Lerner Index can be found in Abba Lerner, *The concept of Monopoly and the Measurement of Monopoly Power*, 1 Rev. Econ. Stud. 157 (1934). *See also*, Robert M Landes & Richard A. Posner, *Market Power in Antitrust Cases* 94 Harv. L. Rev. 937 (1981).
[159] The monopolist's cost at its profit maximizing level of output may differ from the costs that would exist under conditions of perfect competition. Thus, it may not be entirely accurate to say that the ratio is based in the difference between the monopolist's price and costs under competitive conditions. Still, the Index stand as a measure of the monopolist's power to raise prices above its own costs. Landes & Posner, *supra* note 22, at 941.
[160] *Id.* at 940.
[161] Understanding Antitrust and Its Economic Implication, 5th Ed. Ethomas Sullivan & Jeffery L. Harrison. At 28.
[162] 253 F. 3d 34 (D.C. Cir. 2001).

reconciling traditional antitrust economics with the existence of network effects has been

discussed. When there is a network effect the actual attractiveness and usefulness of a product

increases as the number of people using the product increases. In a manner analogous to a natural

monopoly, one might expect the market to evolve eventually to a monopolistic state. Greater

compatibility may follow from one firm having a dominant market share. To put it in economic

terms, consumer surplus may be positively related to dominance by one producer. Also, the

consumer is better off by efforts to use that market power to exact higher prices or to otherwise

stifle the innovation of others.

Furthermore, the Supreme Court has noted that the purpose of market definition is to

assess whether the agreement will have anticompetitive impact.[163] In other words, market

analysis is a means to an end of determining the likely anticompetitive impact. If the impact can

be assessed without a complete market analysis, a court may not require the plaintiff to go

through the market analysis.[164] As the Court reasoned, proof of detrimental effect "can obviate

the need for an inquiry into market power."[165]

B. The Courts' Application of Market Power; case analysis

The application of sound economic principles to a market power analysis has had an

uneven history in the courts. It is not uncommon for a court to approach the market power issue

---

[163] *FTC v. Indiana Federation of Dentists*, 476 U.S. 447 (1986).
[164] *Id.*
[165] *Id.* at 461. *See also National Athletic Ass's v. Board of Regents of the University of Oklahoma*, 468 U.S. 85 (1984).

with a methodology that is consistent with economic theory. Sometimes, these sound instincts break down at the point of application. On the other hand, there is a trend toward greater sophistication among the courts when it comes to market analysis.

a. United States V. Aluminum Company of America (Alcoa)[166]

As I previously discussed, one of the best known casea to determine market share is found in Judge Hand's opinion in *Alcoa*. Even though the court did not apply the current understanding of the variety of factors influencing market power, the case still suggest the understanding of market power application in the court.

The issue was what was Alcoa's market share in the virgin ingot market. Several facts complicated the analysis. First, some ingot was imported. Second, some ingot was manufactured by Alcoa and then fabricated by Alcoa into shapes that were sold. Third, to some extent, ingot could be made from aluminum that was recaptured. This is secondary ingot. In determining that Alcoa's market share was 90%, Judge Hand took a number of controversial steps. First, he excluded from the market, or the denominator of the market share fraction, all foreign produced

---

[166] Explain, on April 23. 1937, in the Federal District Court for the Southern District of New York, the federal government brought a lengthy antitrust complaint against the Aluminum Company of America, seeking the dissolution of that company as a relief to the petition. Four years, 155 witness, 1803 exhibits, and 58,000 trial court pages later, District Court Judge Francis G. Caffey, in an unusual nine-day oral presentation, cleared the firm of all wrongdoing, thought he reserved judgement on two counts. The government had made nearly 140 separate charges involving antitrust violations, supposedly ranging from Aloca's monopolization of bauxite deposits, water power sites, aluminum castings, alumina and virgin ingot aluminum, to the conscious "squeezing" of fabricators and repeated conspiracy with other aluminum firms. Judge Caffey found the firm innocent of all the monopoly and conspiracy charges and dismissed them. On appeal by the government to a special Appeals Court acting in lieu of the U.S. Supreme Court, Judge Learned Hand, speaking for the majority, reversed one of Caffey's judgments and found Aloca guilty of illegally monopolizing virgin ingot aluminum. To comprehend this complex case and the two different judgements, one must place them in the context of the aluminum industry prior to 1937.

ingot expect that sold within the United States. He implicitly recognized the concept of supply

elasticity and the impact foreign production could have on Alcoa's pricing decisions. In fact, he

observed that foreign producers could "immediately . . . divert to the American market what they

have been selling elsewhere."[167] He evidently felt that this supply elasticity was too low to

warrant including the capacity of foreign producers in the United States market due to barriers

created from "the tariff and the cost of transportation."[168] Precisely why these costs would limit

foreign competition as thoroughly as Judge Hand indicated is not clear from the opinion, and it is

likely that the market was drawn too narrowly.[169] Second, Judge Hand also excluded from the

market all secondary ingot. His reasoning was that Alcoa was ultimately in control of the

secondary market. In addition, there were users who found secondary ingot unacceptable

regardless of the price of virgin ingot. In all likelihood, the cost of recycling may have been high

enough to result in a low elasticity of supply. Still, it is unlikely that Alcoa's pricing was

unaffected in control of the amount of secondary aluminum. The fact that Alcoa was ultimately

in control the amount recycled in any one year. Complete exclusion of the secondary market,

may have resulted in an inappropriately narrow market.[170]

b. Eastman Kodak v. Image Technical Services

---

[167] 149 F. 2d at 426.
[168] *Id.*
[169] *See* Richard A. Posner & Frank H. Easterbrook, Antitrust 626-27 (2d ed. 1981).
[170] Professor Landes and Judge Posner suggest that the narrow market definition may have influenced Judge Hand's decision to require high market shares in order for Aloca to be characterized as a monopoly. Landes & Posner, *supra* 22, at 978-79.

With its decision in Eastman Kodak Co. v. Image Technical Services, Inc.,2 the Supreme Court again has attempted to clarify both procedural and substantive antitrust doctrine under sections 1 and 2 of the Sherman Act. For the early part of the tying cases, the Court addressed the substantive law of tying arrangements[171] under section 1 of the Sherman Act[172]. the first thirteen cases proved unlucky for adherents to the University of Chicago school od antitrust theory ("Chicago School") since the economic analysis at the heart of their jurisprudential vision of antitrust enforcement took a back seat to a moderate tone of antitrust theory. Furthermore, the Supreme Court's examination and clarification of section 2[173] doctrine was equally skeptical of Chicago School analysis. The scope and importance of the Kodak decision is the topic of this Comment.

Various factors fostered, or are evidence of, the Chicago School's influential position in the realm of antitrust jurisprudence. The Supreme Court's decision in Continental T.V., Inc. v. GTE Sylvania, Inc.[174] is the most prominent example of Chicago School influence. In Sylvania, the Court explicitly overruled the per se prohibition of vertical non-price restraints articulated only ten years previously in United States v. Arnold, Schwinn & Co.[175] In doing so, the Court endorsed the viewpoints of various Chicago School theorists.[176]

---

[171] A tying arrangement is "an agreement by a party to sell one product but only on the condition that the buyer also purchase a different (or tied) product, or at least agrees that he will not purchase that product from any other supplier." *Northern Pac Ry.*, 356 U.S at 5-6.

[172] 15 U.S.C. § 1 (1988). The relevant portion of § 1 states that: "Every contract, combination in the form of trust or otherwise, or conspiracy, in restraint of trade or commerce among the several States, or with foreign nations, is declared to be illegal."

[173] 15 U.S.C. § 2 (1988). The relevant portion of the section states: "Every person who shall monopolize, or attempt to monopolize, or combine or conspire with any other person or persons, to monopolize any part of the trade or commerce among the several States, or with foreign nations, shall be deemed guilty of a felony . . . ." *Id.*

[174] 433 U.S. 36 (1977). Facing decreasing market share and significant foreign competition, Sylvania had adopted policies designed to recruit more aggressive and competent retailers.

[175] 388 U.S. 365 (1967).

[176] In the course of its opinion, the Court repeatedly cited Richard A. Posner, Antitrust Policy and the Supreme Court: An Analysis of the Restricted Distribution, Horizontal Merger and Potential Competition Decisions, 75 COLUM. L. REV. 282 (1975). Sylvania, 433 U.S. at 48 n.13, 51 n.18, 53 n.21, 55, 56, 56 n.24. The Court also cited

When the Supreme court grant certiorari[177], many members of the antitrust bar thought Kodak might further expand the influence of the Chicago School. After the Supreme Court affirmed the Ninth Circuit's denial of defendant's summary judgment motion, the reaction from practitioners and scholars was swift and varied. Also, the various issues addressed by the Supreme Court in Kodak merit such extensive, and contrasting, commentary.

In Kodak, the Supreme Court expressly refused to adopt a new rule of law in tying arrangements,[178] re-examined and restated the appropriate standard for summary judgment in antitrust cases,[179] and possibly signaled the end or limitation of particular jurisprudential assumptions.[180] Finally, though invited to do so by Kodak, the Court never re-examined the efficacy of the per se prohibition against tying. This surprised those who assumed Kodak would be the per se rule's cease.

C. Market Definition

---

other Chicago theorists besides Posner. See, eg., id. at 56 (citing Robert H. Bork, The Rule of Reason and the Per & Concept. Price Fixing and Market Division (pt. 2), 75 YALE LJ..373 (1966)).

[177] Eastman Kodak Co. v. Image Tech. Serv., Inc., 111 S. Ct. 2823 (1991).

[178] The Court characterized Kodak's argument as "urg[ing] the adoption of a substantive legal rule that 'equipment competition precludes any finding of monopoly power in derivative aftermarkets.'" Kodak, 112 S. Ct. at 2082 (citing Petitioner's Brief at 33, Kodak (No. 90-1029); see infra Part IV.

[179] The Court, in discussing its leading antitrust summary judgment case, Matsushita Elec. Indus. Co. v. Zenith Radio Corp., 475 U.S. 574 (1986), held that its "requirement in Matsushita that the plaintiffs' claims make economic sense did not introduce a special burden on plaintiffs facing summary judgment in antitrust cases." Kodak, 112 S. Ct. at 2083; see infra text accompanying notes 223-61.

[180] The Court stated that "[l]egal presumptions that rest on formalistic distinctions rather than actual market realities are generally disfavored in antitrust law." Kodak, 112 S. Ct. at 2082.

Even though it is not as common as addressing anticompetitive conduct by sellers, a number of antitrust cases arise when buyers combine to set prices or the terms of exchange.[181] When this occurs, the defendants are said to be using monopsony power. Monopsony power can be the result of an agreement, unlawful under Section 1 of the Sherman Act or the result of single firm behavior under Section 2.

Regarding market power, the key in a monopsony case is to assess the market from the point of view of sellers attempting to sell their goods or services. In the monopsony context influences exist that are comparable to demand and supply substitutability.

It may appear that lower prices for inputs paid by a manufacturer could hardly be harmful. First, it should be noted that the antitrust laws are designed to encourage competitive markets in the interest of allocative efficiency. The use of monopsony power, much like the use of monopoly power, prevents the market from working to allocate resources to their most valued uses. Second, the fact that a firm may pay less for an input does not mean that the savings will be passed on to consumers. Lower input prices may mean that producers of the inputs supply less and the output of the final product is lower and prices actually increase.

In 2007 the United State Supreme Court addressed the monopsony question in *Weyerhaeuser Co. v. Ross-Simmons Hardwood Lumber Co.*[182] The issue was what standard should be applied in the context of an allegation that a firm had engaged in predatory bidding. The Court noted that a monopsonist has the power to lower the price of inputs. Due to the posture of the case there was no opportunity for the Court to analyze the determinants of market

---

[181] *See, e,g., Fraser V. Major League Soccer*, 284 F.3d 47 (1st Cir. 2002); *Todd v. Exxon Corp.*, 275 F.3d
[182] 127 S.Ct. 1069 (2007).

power, but it did note the "close theoretical connection between monopoly and monopsony."[183] This would mean adopting the point of view of sellers and identifying alternative customers to whom their output could be sold.

D. Department of Justice and Federal Trade Commission Guidelines

As I previously discussed, in 1992 the Department of Justice and the Federal Trade Commission released Guidelines pertaining to enforcement policy with respect to mergers. The same Guidelines are not necessarily applicable to the enforcement of Section 2 of the Sherman Act. Nor does the issuance of the Guidelines mean that they will be applied by courts considering Section 2 offenses. The Guidelines are noteworthy, however, because the actual process of arriving at the relevant market helps illuminate the economic relationships that influence market power.

With respect to the product market definition, the objective is to determine a group of products such that a hypothetical firm that was the only present and future seller of those products could profitably impose a small but significant and nontransitory increase in price. With respect to the geographic market definition, the goal is also to identify the geographic boundaries of a hypothetical firm selling the relevant products that could profitably raise prices.

In both instances, the agency starts with the product and geographic market of the firm under question and assumes a small price increase in order to determine if other firms would

---

[183] 275 F.3d 191 (2d Cir. 2001).

74

respond. If the response, in terms of substitute products or shifting of products from other locations, is great enough to make the price increase unprofitable, those producers or locations are added to the market in ascertaining the defendant's market share.

Even though it may vary from market to market, the basic definition of a small but significant and nontransitory price increase is a 5% increase lasting a year. The change in price in seen as made at prevailing prices. Since the Guidelines are designed for merger analysis, there is no indication of what market share would be sufficiently high to lead to an inference that the defendant possessed the required monopoly power in a Section 2 case. However, the general market definition methodology is relatively liberal with respect to the inclusion of the productive capacity of competitors or potential competitors in the defendant's market. If all other factors remain constant, when applied to Section 2 cases, the approach would result in relatively few instances in which firms are found to possess monopoly power.

Chapter V. Reconcile the Confliction between IP and Antitrust

The significant distinguish between intellectual property from property is that it regards information. Intellectual Property is not only intangible, but also it is considered as a public good. Thus Intellectual property present different problems than real and chattel property.

For at least the past century, the intersection of competition and intellectual property laws has presented difficult issues for courts and commentators. Although the two systems attempt to increase total societal welfare, they pursue this goal through different paths. The foundation of the IP system is the right to exclude. Such a right is designed to allow innovators to charge prices high enough to recover their investment costs and gain profits, thereby encouraging future innovation.

The exclusion at the core of IP may nonetheless be punished under the competition laws, such as antitrust laws. These laws scrutinize activity that restricts competition, because such conduct could lead to higher prices, lower output, and often less innovation. Monopolists, typically lack the constraints provided by competitive markets. Similarly, by their very nature, agreement between IP holders and licensees restrict competition.

On a larger scale, owners could combine their IP. Patentees could jointly set royalties for multiple patents in a patent pool. Copyright holders could offer blanket licenses that provide access to numerous copyrighted works. And IP owners could enter into joint venture and mergers. This broad range of activity may make perfect sense from the standpoint if dispersing or exploiting the protected innovation. However, the greater need for cooperation from the perspective of IP law could trigger the suspicion of the competition law.

Since the passage of the Sherman Act in 1890, US courts have been left to reconcile these two systems without any compass to guide them. As a result, their analysis of IP and competition issues has shifted dramatically. In the period immediately following the enactment of the Sherman Act, courts treated IP as paramount. By the middle of the 20th century, they had adopted an approach hostile to IP. By the 1980s, the pendulum had swung back, with courts deferring once again to IP.

From the vantage point in the early 21st century, much of competition law's deference to IP is beneficial and most significantly has reduced the saliency of the IP-Antitrust conflict.

However, as the history of the intersection in the 20th century reveals, this has been a difficult way.

1. The Court's Treatments of IP and Antitrust

In The Antitrust Enterprise, Herbert Hovenkamp offeres one of the most exhaustive treatments of the history of IP and antirust.[184] Hovenkamp explains that 'over the years the court has claimed to find many conflicts between the competition-furthering policies of the antitrust laws and the protection of exclusive rights that the IP laws afford'. However, he asserts that 'many of these conflicts were imagined' since some courts 'condemned and IP practice... without asking whether the practice threatened competition in any important way' while other courts 'exonerated an anticompetitive practice without a clear indication that the practice was necessary... to protect a legitimate IP right'.[185]

In the period from 1890 to 1912 the court refused to impose antitrust liablity for patent-based activity. They treated IP as under the owners' discretion. For example, in E. Bement & Sons v. National Harrow Co.[186], the Supreme Court upheld price fixing among competitors who held IP, explaining that 'the very object of the patent laws is monopoly' and that 'any conditions which are not in their very nature illegal... will be upheld by the courts'.[187] Hoevnkamp also discussed A.B. Dick v. Henry[188], in which the Court upheld a tying arrangement that required

---

[184] Hovenkamp, Herbert. The antitrust enterprise. Harvard University Press, 2009.
[185] *Id.*
[186] 47 NYS 462 (1897).
[187] *Id.*
[188] 224 U.S. 1 (1912).

those who wished to license a patented machine to use certain unpatented supplies, concluding

that 'arrangements based on suggestions of public policy not recognized in the patent law are not

relevant'.[189]

Congress responded to the Court's decision in A.B Dick by enacting the Clayton Act,

which prohibited the tying of patented and unpatented products. At around the same time, courts

began to limit the power of patentees. In Motion Picture Patents Co. v. Universal Film

Manufacturing expand the patent monopoly beyond the scope of the patented item and that

patentees' rights flowed not from patent law but from the 'general law of the ownership of …

property'.[190]

Hovemkamp also explains how the court initially relied on the doctrine of patent misuse

in imposing limits on patentees.[191] In Carbice Corp. of America v. American Patents

Development Corp.[192], the Court denied a contributory infringement claim brought by a patentee

that had required users seeking patented products to buy unpatented products on the grounds that

a patent could not be utilized to 'secure a limited monopoly of unpatented material used in

applying the invention'.[193] The court explicitly relied on antitrust principles in Mericoid Corp. v.

Minneapolis-Honeywell Regulator Co[194]., stating that 'the legality of any attempt to bring

unpatented goods within the protection of the patent is measured by the antitrust laws' and that

---

[189] *Id.*
[190] 243 U.S. 502, 510 (1917). This approach continues to be followed by courts. See Ethyl Gasoline Corp. v. United States, 309 U.S. 436, 456 (1940) ("The extent of that right is limited by the definition of his invention, as its boundaries are marked by the specifications and claims of the patent."); United States v. Studiengesellschaft Kohle, m.b. H., 670 F. 2d 1122, 1135 (D.C. Cir. 1981) ("None of the anticompetitive effects of the challenged restriction … exceed the anticompetitive effects which the patent authorized.").
[191] Hovenkamp, *supra* note 159.
[192] 283 U.S. 27 (1931).
[193] *Id.*
[194] 320 US 680, 684 (1944);

'the effort … made to control competition in an unpatented device plainly violates the antitrust laws'.[195]

In the mid-20th century, the Supreme Court adopted an even more aggressive stance toward IP. Three examples reveal its hostile treatment of patent ties, cross-licensing agreements, territorial restraints, and other arrangements. In International Salt Co. v. United States[196], the Court found a tying arrangement to be per se illegal, and refused to analyze the issue of market power since 'the tendency of the arrangement to accomplishment of monopoly seems obvious'.[197] In United State v. Loew's[198], the Court struck down 'block booking', by which a party conditions the license or sale of desired movies on the buyer's acceptance of a package containing unwanted films, explaining that 'the requisite economic power is presumed when the tying product is patented or copyrighted'.[199] Finally, in United States v. Line Material Co.[200], the Court attacked cross-licensing arrangements as price fixing even though the public could 'obtain the full benefit of the efficiency and economy of the inventions' only by using both products.[201]

Aligned with the Court's increasingly hostile approach to tying and cross-licensing arrangements were the 'Nine No-No's', announced by the Department of Justice Antitrust Division in 1970 and followed for approximately a decade. The Nine No-No's encompassed IP licensing activities that the agency regarded as suspect under the antitrust laws. The list included nine activities, including tying, grantbacks, and mandatory package licensing, which often did not harm competition.

---

[195] *Id.*
[196] 332 U.S. 392 (1947)[
[197] *Id.*
[198] 371 U.S. 38 (1962).
[199] *Id.*
[200] 333 U.S. 287 (1948).
[201] *Id.*

In the 1970s courts began to follow a more economics-based approach, analyzing the competitive effects of business arrangements. Scholars affiliated with the Chicago School of Economics played a pivotal role in the transformation.

One of the crucial cases of this period was Continental T.V., Inc. v. GTE Sylvania, Inc.[202] In this case, the Supreme Court examined whether a territorial restraint, by which a manufacturer limits a franchisee to a particular area, violated Section 1 of the Sherman Act. The Court discarded a formalistic approach that had depended on whether title to the object had been transferred, and focused instead on the market effect of the restrictions.[203] It particularly concerned their ability to stimulate interbrand competition between different manufacturers. This holding had a significant effect on IP licensing arrangements, which often take the form of nonprice vertical restraints and which are nearly always upheld today.

Another case strengthening IP's position was BMI Music Inc. v. Columbia Broadcasting, Inc.,[204] in which the Court analyzed blanket licenses that allowed licensees to perform any of millions of copyrighted musical works in a package. Although there was an element of price fixing in the arrangement, the Court held that rule of reason analysis applied given the license's benefits in creating a product that would not otherwise have been available.

In addition to these two cases, courts consistently upheld parties' activities in introducing new products. In Berkey Photo, Inc. v. Eastman Kodak Co., for instance, the court refused to punish Kodak's failure to 'predisclose' its product to competitors. It explained that 'withholding … advance knowledge of one's new products … ordinarily constitutes valid competitive

---

[202] 433 U.S. 36 (1977).
[203] Id.
[204] 441 U.S. 1 (1979).

conduct'. The court recognized that a contrary rule that compelled a firm to share the benefits of 'risky and expensive R&D would vitiate innovation incentives'. Courts also refused to punish firms that introduced new products that had the effect of injuring competitors. They found that IBM could redesign its product 'to make them more attractive to buyers' rather than 'constricting its product development so as to facilitate sales of rival products'.[205]

Legislation also contributed to IP deference. The Federal Courts Improvement Act of 1982 created the Federal Circuit, the sole appellate court to decide patent cases, which brought about a more predictable and uniform patent law than the 'expensive, time-consuming and unseemly forum-shopping' that had characterized patent litigation.[206] The National Cooperative Research Act of 1984 required antitrust courts to consider joint ventures engaging in R&D under the rule of reason, thus encouraging collaborations.[207] Also, as Hovenkamp explains, the Patent Misuse Reform Act of 1988 made it clear that a refusal to license a patented item and the tying of a patented good to a second product where the inventor lacked market power in the tying product did not constitute misuse.[208]

The transition to the increasing dominance of IP doctrine was crystallized in 1995 when the antitrust agencies issued the Antitrust Guidelines for the Licensing of Intellectual Property. The Guidelines embodied three principles, 1) IP is 'essentially comparable' to any other form of

---

[205] *Id.*

[206] Petrowitz, Harold C. "Federal Court Reform: The Federal Courts Improvement Act of 1982--And Beyond." Am. UL Rev. 32 (1982).

[207] Wright, Christopher OB. "The National Cooperative Research Act of 1984: A New Antitrust Regime for Joint Research and Development Ventures." High Technology Law Journal 1.1 (1986).

[208] Hovenkamp, supra note 159.

property, 2) IP does not automatically create market power in the antitrust context, and 3) IP licensing is generally procompetitive.[209]

These three principles demolished a 50-year history of hostility to IP in American antitrust enforcement. First, they made clear that IP should not be treated more harshly than real property, concluding that IP is not 'particularly suspect' under the antitrust laws. Second, the Guidelines confirmed that even though the IP right 'confers the power to exclude with respect to the specific product, process, or work in question, there will often be sufficient actual or potential close substitutes for such product, process, or work to prevent the exercise of market power'. Third, they explained that licensing 'can lead to more efficient exploitation' of IP, benefiting consumers by reducing costs, promoting R&D investment, and introducing new products.[210]

2. Application of New Economic Concepts

In the 21st century, one hotly debated issue has been whether US competition law can apply to the new economy. Also, it is an important issue whether the Sherman Act, enacted in 1890 to address the steel and oil industries, can still be relevant in today's modern economy.

Most commentators have reasonably answered this question in the affirmative. US antitrust law employs a flexible analysis that is able to consider the characteristics of various industries. In the past three decades, antitrust courts have embraced more economics-based analysis that can incorporate new economic characteristics. They have also replaced Per se Rule

---

[209] Hayslett III, Thomas L. "1995 Antitrust Guidelines for the Licensing of Intellectual Property: Harmonizing the Commercial Use of Legal Monopolies with the Prohibition of Antitrust Law." (1995).
[210] *Id.*

that automatically invalidated certain activities with a rule of reason framework that allows consideration of market-specific conditions. In addition, the antitrust agencies have offered nuanced analyses in issuing, for examples, the IP Guidelines and business review letters analyzing patent pools.

When Posner discussed economic application of Antitrust and IP, he broadly refers to computer software, internet-based business, and communications. Specially, Posner discusses the characteristics of the economic application, such as falling average costs, modest capital requirements, high rates of innovation, quick and frequent entry and exit, and network effects, though he recognizes that such power is less durable in high-technology industries. Posner believes that antitrust doctrine is 'sufficiently supple' to cope with the economic concepts, but contends that the 'troublesome' issue lies in institutional enforcement. Thus, Posner advocates the use of neutral competence experts, including a 'technical committee composed of two party-nominated and one neutral technical expert' that would assist a judge in administering a consent or litigated decree. He addresses timelines issues by proposing an 'agreed-upon narrative of the relevant facts' jointly prepared by the parties, with trials limited to disputed issues.[211] In addition, Pitofsky, in Antitrust and Intellectual Property: Unresolved Issues at the Heart of the New Economy, Pitofsky highlights the near-inevitable monopoly that arises from the combination of IP and network effects, though he recognize that such power is less durable in high-technology industries. Pitofsky insists that enforcement 'has generally evolved in recent years in a way that pays heed to the distinctive characteristics of the New Economy'. In supporting this proposition, he points to Federal Trade Commission actions in the 1990s that involved patent settlements,

---

[211] Boudreaux, Donald J. "The second edition of Judge Posner's Antitrust Law: A tempered appreciation." The Antitrust Source (2002).

refusals to license, standard setting, and mergers. Pitofsky also applauds the speed with which the government agencies review nearly all mergers, though he recognizes the desirability of improvement in the non-merger area.[212]

3. Economic Approaches With Regards to the Conflict between IP and Competition

The conflicting relationship between IP and competition law has elicited a vast amount of commentary. Many of the earliest reactions to the conflict involved simply avoiding it altogether, a tendency that continues to the present. Several approaches using formalistic tests, suggested which practices are desirable. Among these approaches, the tests proposed by Bowman and Boxter is considered as the most extensive and thoughtful works to reconcile the conflicts. Both works attempt to develop a consistent framework and to apply it in a variety of contexts in which the IP-antitrust conflict arises.

A. William Baxter

In Legal Restrictions on Exploitation of the Patent Monopoly: An Economic Analysis, Baxter offers the comprehensive reconcilable approach with regard to the conflicting issues on IP and Antitrust. Baxter proposes a test that 'a patentee is entitled to extract monopoly income by

---

[212] See generally, Pitofsky, Robert. "Antitrust and intellectual property: unresolved issues at the heart of the new economy." Berk. Tech. LJ 16 (2001): 535.

restricting utilization of his invention' as long as the restriction is confined 'as narrowly and specifically as the technology of his situation and the practicalities of administration permit'. He applies this test to royalties, tying arrangements, package licensing, price and output limits on licensees, and field and territorial restrictions. He also discusses the difference between legal and economic monopoly, the difficulties of determining reasonable royalties and ascertaining forbidden price discrimination, and the inapplicability of the differential between price and marginal cost at the heat of price discrimination analysis.[213]

Ultimately, he insists that subsidization of innovative activity is probably necessary to achieve the devotion to that activity of an optimum flow of resources. Adoption of the monopoly device for this purpose has the great disadvantage of underutilization of all significant inventions but may be justified by the preference for free market assessment of invention value over administrative assessment. It is essential to market assessment that comparability exist between the benefits that flow to the patentee and the burden imposed upon licensees. If in their bargaining process they are allowed to eternalize the burden of payment by constraints on licensee conduct or by adoption of certain royalty structures, the adverse interest of the licensee no longer serves to check the degree of monopoly and restraint imposed.[214]

Apart from blatant techniques such as the physical destruction of competitors, impairment of comparability occurs through economic arrangements which unnecessarily extend the restraining impact of high price to goods and services other than the invention itself. Some minimal familiarity with price theory is essential to understanding the impact of different arrangement. In particular two economic phenomena recur repeatedly in analysis of licensing

---

[213] See generally, Baxter, William F. "Legal restrictions on exploitation of the patent monopoly: an economic analysis." The Yale Law Journal 76.2 (1966).
[214] *Id.*

problems. One is differential pricing in accordance with demand elasticity, and the other is

arrangement which affect substitution of inputs for the patented input. Because incremental use

of an existing invention is costless, the classic concept of economic discrimination cannot be

applied in this context and with limited exceptions the law should not attempt to control

differential pricing practices. Arrangement which block the substitution for the patented product

of other factor inputs, on the other hand, is a serious problem to which inadequate attention has

been given.

B. Ward Bowman

Ward Bowman assesses various forms of patent licensing in his book, IP and Antitrust

Law: A Legal and Economic Appraisal, and the most cited section of the book is typically

recognized for the assertion that antitrust and IP laws do not conflict. Antitrust law and IP law

are frequently viewed as standing in diametric opposition, because one is promotes competition

and the other is promotes monopoly.[215] However, in terms of the economic goals sought, the

supposed opposition between these laws is lacking. Since both antitrust law and IP law have a

common central economic goal which is to maximize wealth by producing what consumers want

at the lowest cost. In serving this common goal, reconciliation between IP and antitrust law

involves serious problems of assessing effects, but not conflicting purposes. Antitrust law does

not demand competition under all circumstances. Quite properly, it permits monopoly when

monopoly makes for greater output than would the alternative of an artificially fragmented and

---

[215] Bowman, Ward. "Patent and antitrust law: A legal and economic appraisal." (1973).

inefficient industry. The IP monopoly fits directly into this scheme insofar as its central aim is achieved. It is designed to provide something which consumers' value and which they could not have at all or have as abundantly were no IP protection afforded.

Bowman insists a 'common central economic goal' for the two regimes. One is to 'maximize wealth by producing what consumers want at the lowest cost'. The other is elaborating the first concept, he explains that the goal of both laws is to 'maximize allocative efficiency and productive efficiency while minimizing output restriction. More specifically, the goal of both antitrust law and IP law is to maximize allocative efficiency, making what consumers want, and productive efficiency, make these goods with the fewest scare resources.[216] In achieving this goal under either antitrust or IP law the detriment to be avoided is output restriction. This may arise from monopolization which diverts production from more urgent to less urgent use or from legal rules requiring inefficient methods of production. The evil, then may be viewed as net output restriction after efficiency increases are accounted for. Both antitrust and IP law seek output expansion, not output restriction. Competition deserves support insofar as it brings about this result. And so it is with IPs. The temporary monopoly afforded by an IP, once a particular invention has come into being, will have all the output restrictive disabilities of any monopoly. The argument for IP is that without this temporary monopoly there would be insufficient profit incentives to produce the invention, and that because an invention is profitable only if consumers are willing to pay what the patentee charges, the consumers are therefore better off than they would be without the invention, even if they are charged monopoly prices. If this is so, a trade-if, some monopoly restraint for greater output in the long run, is in the

---

[216] *Id.*

87

interest of socially desirable resource allocation.[217] An appraisal of alleged conflicts between

antitrust law and IP law depends upon understanding the role of profits in providing the incentive

for undertaking efficient production of those things consumers value.

C. Louise Kaplow

In contrast to Bowman, in the Patent-Antitrust Intersection: A Reappraisal, Kaplow

explains that the conflict between IP and antitrust law is 'even more deep-seated than is

generally perceived'.[218] One reason is that 'it is wholly indeterminate how any individual case …

should be decided, because the question is whether the totality of the courts' IP-antitrust

decisions promotes an appropriate level of reward. Another reason is that the determination of

IP-antitrust doctrine is linked to the calculation of the optimal IP right life – the 'length of time at

which the marginal social cost of lengthening or shortening the IP right life equals the marginal

social benefit' – which itself presents challenging issues.

However, he nonetheless offers the reconcilable analysis of a 'ratio' test that is the most

comprehensive analysis of the intersection yet offered.[219] The test examines the ratio between

---

[217] If this is so, it is not because the trade-restraining effect is beneficial, rather it is because correcting the restraint would involve greater cost (in the form id misdirected resources elsewhere) than would be saved by eliminating the particular restraint (see Williamson, "Economies as an Antitrust Defense: The Welfare Trade-offs," 58 Am. Econ. Rev. 18 (March 1968). This is an example of what antitrust law recognize as an "ancillary restraint"- one necessary to the achievement of a greater gain elsewhere. Even with trade-offs, however, economic assessment is in terms of output-a search for more output, overall, of the things consumers prefer.

[218] Louise Kaplow, the Patent Antitrust Intersection: A Reappraisal, 97 HARV. L. REV. 1813 (1984).

[219] Ratio test can be define as:

Patentee Reward

Monopoly Loss

In this ratio, 'patentee reward' and 'monopoly loss' refer, respectively, to the incremental reward and loss resulting from the practice in question. In general the higher the ratio the more desirable the practice. In addition, the ratio test may be used to determine the desirability not only of restrictive practices, which are the subject of patent-antitrust 'the reward the owner of IP rights receives when permitted to use a particular restrictive practice'[220] and 'the monopoly loss that results from such exploitation of the IP rights'. Kaplow applies the test to an array of activity, including patent-restricted licenses, patent combinations, price discrimination, and patentee control of unpatented end products.

4. Proposed Solutions and the Criticism under Economic Concepts

A. Bowman's 'competitive superiority' Test and Criticism

Bowman states that his test 'assumes the propriety of allowing a patentee to use any method of charging what the traffic will bear if, but only if, the reward to the patentee arising from the conditional use measures the patented product's competitive superiority over substitutes.'[221] This competitive superiority approach has two components. Primarily, Bowman relies on an objective test that takes an affirmative evidence of legitimacy a licensee's or buyer's willingness to accept a restriction as a condition to the deal. Bowman does not completely limit himself to this objective component, because it would potentially immunize any restrictive practice by a patentee, even a blatant cartel. Instead, Bowman sometimes proceeds beyond the

---

doctrine, but also of changes in the patent life itself. Every patent life implies a specific ratio. The ratio implicit in a given patent life simply refers to the ratio of incremental reward to incremental loss that results from a marginal adjustment in the patent life.

[220] The common view that restrictive practices should be evaluated by determining whether the resulting reward exceeds the value of the patent is misguided. In general, the reward should be less than the value of the patent, and even this requirement is not a sufficient condition for the desirability of permitting a given practice. Rather, the determinative inquiry is that indicated by the ratio test, whether the resulting marginal increase in reward is substantial by comparison to the marginal increase in monopoly loss, and how that ratio compares to the ratios for other restrictive practices and for the existing patent life.

[221] Bowman, *supra* note 216.

objective test of what the market will bear. Therefore, he must be considering some additional limitation when he refers to 'competitive superiority.' Moreover, it must be addressed in every case, even if his principle is rarely dispositive. Bowman seems to rely upon formalistic conceptions like a characterizing the pure cartel as a 'scope extension'. For instance, he reasons that "evaluating whether certain patent licensing practices should be sanctioned will involve the proper scope of the legal monopoly. Is more being monopolized than what the patent grants, or is the practice merely maximizing the reward attributable to the competitive advantage afforded by a patent?"[222] One reason the indeterminacy of Bowman's test may not readily present itself upon first reading is that pure horizontal cartelization is virtually the only behavior he would prohibit. Because it is generally agreed element of his position, the reader might be lulled into accepting it uncritically.

In addition to Bowman's ambiguous language, there is a further obstacle to understanding and analyzing his test. In most contexts, he finds his test to be satisfied a fortiori, because he believes that most allegedly restrictive practices should not be held to violate the antitrust laws even in the absence of patent policy considerations. These beliefs, which Bowman shares with others in the 'Chicago School,' derive form criticisms of arguments based upon leverage, foreclosure, and exclusionary practices. To the extent that Bowman's argument rests upon such beliefs, his book adds nothing to the resolution of the patent-antitrust conflict. This Article devotes little attention to these issues and instead concentrates on how the patent-antitrust conflict should be resolved when some conflict is found to exist. Because Bowman so rarely finds anything worthy of concern from the antitrust side of the conflict, most of his discussion of the conflict is only tangentially relevant if one regards the antitrust issues to be of central

---

[222] *Id.*

concern. Nonetheless, his previously quoted statement of the competitive superiority test, combined with his frequent passing references to and applications of the test, seem sufficient to allow an understanding of the rule he intends.

Kaplow criticize that Bownan's competitive superiority test and formalistic component principle fail to resolve the patent-antitrust conflict satisfactorily. Even if one leaves aside the problems of defining 'competitive superiority,' one can readily perceive the short-comings of his objective test, upon which he normally relies, by comparing it with the ratio test.[223] Bowman also misunderstands the connection between setting the optimal patent life and determining patent-antitrust doctrine. He states that "lengthening or shortening the patent period seems a far better solution to the rewarding problem than is manipulating patent exploitation standards."[224] Of course, any given set of patent-antitrust doctrine can be termed a 'manipulation' only by reference to some unbiased starting point. Bowman's reference point is, in fact, quite biased in that it is derived from a one-sided analysis. More fundamentally, ratio test demonstrated that the problem of rewarding patentees inevitably combines analysis of the patent period and patent-antitrust doctrine in manner that undercuts Bowman's position.

Bowman's test seems to focus solely on the numerator of the ratio like the patentee's reward. From this perspective, the test permits any reward to the patentee that does not exceed the bound set by 'competitive superiority.' By permitting any restrictive practice that the licensee or buyer is willing to endure, it implicitly compares the situation in which the practice is permitted to that in which the invention had never existed, or, equivalently, to the situation in

---

[223] The ration test, which compares the patentee's reward to the monopoly loss imposed on society, should guide the evaluation of restrictive practices. Practices with higher ratios generally should be preferred. Factors aiding in the application of this test to specific practices include the extent to which the reward is pure transfer, the portion of the reward that accrues to the patentee, and the degree to which the reward serves as an incentive.
[224] W. Bowman, PATENT AND ANTUTRUST LAW 118 (1973), at 52; see id . at 115

which the patentee refuses to practice the patent.[225] Thus Bowman's test can be seen as another version of the argument that the greater includes the lesser, which was seen to ignore the antitrust side of the conflict. The test is flawed because it ignores the denominator. Because, Bowman presents the conclusion that various restrictions "are all means not of creating monopoly, but rather of maximizing the return the patent affords."[226] He is correct that the restrictions probably help maximize the patentee's rewards (the numerator), but the reference to 'creating monopoly' seems more germane to the magnitude of the denominator (monopoly loss). Bowman thus appears in this instance to assert a conclusion concerning the magnitude of the denominator based solely upon the magnitude of the numerator, in effect treating them as if they were mutually exclusive categories. This is clearly incorrect, because the numerator and denominator generally tend to move together.

When discussing the economics of the patent system more generally, Bowman takes notice of both the system's costs and benefits. "The problem should thus be recognized as involving a trade-off between the short-run disadvantages of monopoly on already granted patents and the possibly greater advantages of having new or better products not otherwise available."[227] However, Bowman's test does not take account of this trade-off. As a result, he does not compare the cost of various practices with an eye toward providing incentive at the lowest cost possible. In short, his approach erroneously assumes that, but for the reward provided by each restrictive practice he advocates, none of the invention that the patentees exploit would have been forthcoming. The cost component thus is ignored when he examines the patent-antitrust conflict.

---

[225] *Id* at 88.
[226] *Id* at 55-56.
[227] *Id* at 17.

Although it was noted previously that the numerator and denominator, such as patentee reward and monopoly loss, tend to vary together, it was established that the connection is quite loose. Moreover, it was noted that even if the connection were perfect, there would be no basis for determinately resolving any component of patent-antitrust doctrine. Merely knowing that the numerator is not too large in any given instance does not allow one to decide whether the restriction at issue is better or worse than most others. At best, such knowledge has some bearing on the notion that reward should be proportional to the value of the patent. This information would be sufficient for an application of the proportionality test, but that test was shown in his analysis to be inadequate.[228]

The limit imposed by the competitive superiority test, what the market will bear, is not totally unrelated to the magnitude of the denominator. If the denominator is sufficiently large, the traffic may not bear the restriction. Even with this refinement, however, the competitive superiority test is inadequate. The buyer's or licensee's decision to accept a deal depends tells us neither how much of the buyer's or licensee's cost accrues to the patentee as reward nor how

---

[228] Optimization through equating marginal cost and benefit will yield some average proportion between reward to the patentee and value of the patent. But that relationship, which refers to average rather than marginal conditions, is an informational by-product of the optimization process that has no direct relevance in determining the appropriateness of particular restrictive practices. The proportionality approach implicitly begins by picking a proportion between reward and value and then uses the proportion as a decision rule. This process is both conceptually backwards and, because the proportion is typically assumed to equal one, wrong in its outcome.

Moreover, using a proportion of less than one is of little help. Such an approach offers no answer to the conceptual question of how such a proportion should be chosen. In addition, the proportionality test is easy to apply only when the proportion equals to deal with the patentee implies that the reward is less than the value of the patent. Such an observation demonstrates only that the proportion is less than one. It offers no basis for the inference that the proportion is less than some number smaller than one. The latter inference requires far more detailed information concerning not only the rewards, but also the value of the patent. The value of the patent could prove most difficult to determine. The problems posed by the lack of information. For instance, to determine ratios for particular practice, a number of complicated phenomena must be measured and compared. And if more than a minor reshuffling through cost-effectiveness analysis is desired, it is also necessary to have information concerning the ratio implicit in the existing patent life, which in turn requires detailed knowledge about all the links in the relationship between the patent life and the costs and benefits of the patent system. Moreover, even if the total benefits and total costs could be easily approximated, these approximate values would be virtually useless. It is necessary to know the marginal costs and benefits and the degree of reward that can be inferred from them, and these marginal effects will be much harder to estimate.

much deterrent results, such as monopoly loss. For instance, individual may accept the conditions knowing that, if they do not, others will. Of the conditions are outlawed, however, the patentee may come forward with a better offer. This is not to say that under such circumstances the result is always preferable, for the patentee no doubt receives less benefit. The point instead is that one would have to consider all these effects in order to determine the ratio, which in turn would guide the decision concerning whether the conditions should be permitted. Therefore, the purpose of the ratio test is to incorporate precisely these questions.

Bowman's 'competitive superiority' test allows a patentee to utilize a restrictive practice of the reward to the patentee measures "the patented product's competitive superiority over substitutes."[229] While such a test recognizes the benefits produced by the patent system and the role played by profit maximization, it does not calculate the net effect of a patent's competitive superiority. That is, the cost of the patent system, in the form of monopoly loss that accompanies patentees' elimination of competition, is not considered.[230]

Also, Bowman accords substantial weight to the scope of the patent, stating that the evaluation of licensing practices "will involve the proper scope of the legal monopoly."[231] Consequently, practices will be upheld if they "merely maximize the reward attributable to the competitive advantage afforded by a patent" but prohibited if "more is being monopolized than what the patent grant."[232] Thus, the issues of patent scope does not provide the answer to the patent-antitrust conflict. Because of the emphasis on patent scope and the failure to consider the

---

[229] See *generally*, W. Bowman, PATENT AND ANTUTRUST LAW, (1973).
[230] See *Supra* note 225, at 88, For instance, Bowman considers a licensee's payment to a patentee as evidence of the competitive superiority of the license (if it were not superior, so the argument goes, the licensee would not agree to it) without considering the costs concomitantly imposed by the patentee. In addition, the determination of the patent's competitive superiority over substitutes threatens to be plagued by problems of administration.
[231] See *Supra* note 225, at 8-9.
[232] See *Supra* note 225, at 9.

costs of the patent monopoly. Therefore, Bowman's test fails to accord a sufficient role to antitrust.

B. Baxter's 'comparability' test and the Criticism

William Baxter offers a 'comparability' test that provides that 'a patentee is entitled to extract monopoly income by restricting utilization of his invention' as long as the restriction is confined 'as narrowly and specifically as the technology of his situation and the practicalities of administration permit.'[233] Baxter wisely avoids reliance on more conclusory test, like the purpose of the patentee or the direct nature of the restraint. And his test recognizes that other goods and services might be affected by the exploitation of the patent. He explains that "a patentee is entitled to extract monopoly income by restricting utilization of his invention, notwithstanding that utilization of other goods and services are consequently restricted."[234]

Baxter's test is that

a patentee is entitled to extract monopoly income by restricting utilization of his invention, notwithstanding that utilization of other goods and services are consequently restricted, provided that in each case he confines the restriction to his invention as

---

[233] William F. Baxter, Legal Restrictions on Exploitation of the Patent Monopoly: An Economic Analysis, 76 YALE L.J. 267, at 313 (1966).
[234] Id.

narrowly and specifically as the technology of his situation and the practicalities of administration permit.[235]

This test seems remarkably similar to the formalistic test that inquire into the 'scope of the patent.' One possible interpretation of Baxter's test is that it is concerned primarily with limiting the reward to the patentee. In fact, Baxter states that his formulation is desirable because it provides "a stream of benefits to the patentee ... roughly comparable to the ultimate value of the invention."[236] Thus this 'comparability' test is similar with Bowman's 'comparative superiority' test. To the extent that this similarity holds the similar central criticism that it ignores the cost of providing the reward. This apparent congruence is not too surprising, because Bowman's test could also be characterized as simply restating the 'scope of the patent' formulation.

However, Bowman and Baxter reach strikingly different conclusions from their similar points of departure. Baxter's language seems more restrictive in terms of the limits it would place on patent exploitation. Unlike Bowman's test, Baxter's does not permit the patentee all that the traffic will bear, but rather requires that restrictions be confined as narrowly as possible. The basis for this further limitation is never clear, although arguably it reflects a bias toward minimizing the infringement upon antitrust policy. Of course, one could just as easily take Baxter's test as the starting point and characterize Bowman's test as one that is biased against antitrust policy. Thus, this dual possibility highlights the emptiness of formalistic attempts to

---

[235] Baxter, Legal Restrictions on Exploitation of the Patent Monopoly: An Economic Analysis, 76 YALE L.J. 267, 297 (1966)
[236] *Id.*

resolve the patent-antitrust conflict. Moreover, even if one assumes that Baxter's test is more restrictive than Bowman's, the criticism leveled against Bowman's test remains applicable. At best, each commentator offers a test regulating the maximum reward without offering any analysis that bears on whether the level selected is anywhere near the appropriate amount or whether that reward is achieved in the least costly manner possible. Moreover, even if the total reward were approximately correct, it might be achieved in an inefficient fashion because no attention is given to whether those restrictions that are permitted have the best ratios and thus result in the least cost.

Also, Baxter's test could be seen as an approach directed at minimizing monopoly loss, the denominator of the ratio, because his focus is on minimizing restriction of the greatest extent possible. Baxter's analysis of many specific applications supports this interpretation. Thus, Baxter's approach can be characterized as one that tends toward results favoring the antitrust side of the conflict, whereas Bowman's tends to favor the patent side. It means that Baxter's test of subject to essentially the same criticism as that lodged against Bowman's test that concentrating exclusively in the denominator is a prior no better than concentrating only on the numerator.

Baxter fails to examine in any systematic way the relationship between patentee reward and monopoly loss. He simply asserts that his formulation "give appropriate scope to both antitrust and patent policy."[237] Yet he offers no reason whatsoever demonstrating that his test yields the correct balance between the total reward patentees receive and the total monopoly loss incurred by society, nor does he demonstrate why his test reliably assesses the desirability of particular restrictions.

---

[237] *Id.*

Therefore, analysis under the ratio test shows that past approaches to the patent-antitrust conflict have been misguided. By ignoring the conflict, by approaching to empty formalisms, or by concentrating on only one component of the ratio, each attempt has failed to address fully the concerns relevant to a determination of proper patent-antitrust policy.

In conclusion, it emphasizes antitrust law, in particular, the minimization of monopoly loss, while down-playing concepts of patentee reward and inventive activity. Baxter's test requires that the restrictions imposed by the patentee be confined "as narrowly and specifically" as possible, the test chips away at the bundle of patent rights without considering the net benefit to society of the patent.[238]

Thus, Such test naturally leads to post hoc second-guessing of the licensing practice utilized by the patentee. Similar to the 'less restrictive alternatives' analysis that antitrust courts use in considering the validity of agreements under the rule of reason, by which courts always can unearth a less restrictive alternative than the restraint invoked. Courts invariably can question licensing restrictions, opining that they could have been even narrower. This concern is heightened based on the flexibility of the factors that courts are to consider under Baxter's test, from "the technology of the patentee's situation" to "the practicalities of administration."[239]

In addition, the test recalls analysis based on the scope of the patent. If the activity is confined "narrowly and specifically enough."[240] In other words, it appears not to extend too far beyond the patent grant, then it is acceptable. However, the issue of patent scope is frequently disputed, not exogenously defined, and susceptible to confusion with market boundary

---

[238] *Id.*
[239] Baxter, *Supra* note 225, at 88, 313.
[240] *Id.*

determinations. Thus the test introduces substantial administrability problems. For every challenged licensing agreement in every industry, courts must examine the relevant technology and practicalities of administration in determining whether the particular type of restriction utilized by the patentee is excessive.

5. Kaplow's 'Ratio' Test as the Most Comprehensive Analysis

Louis Kaplow's 'ratio' test examines the ratio between "the reward the patentee receives when permitted to use a particular restrictive practice" and "the monopoly loss that results from such exploitation of the patent."[241] Licensing practice with higher ratios "generally should be preferred."[242] This formulation solves many of the problems of the Baxter and Bowman approaches. As opposed to the Baxter analysis, which focuses on the monopoly loss accompanying a licensing practice, and the Bowman test, which emphasizes the gross benefit of the patented product, Kaplow's 'ratio' test addresses both halves of the equation. It thereby offers the most nuanced and rigorously developed approach to the patent-antitrust intersection.

However, the Kaplow's test is not perfect. First the level on which it analysis the challenged practice it too specific to be applied practically. Second, the goal of social welfare that serves, in effect, as the common denominator of the analysis also limits the test's applicability. Third, the input the test seeks to maximize is patentee reward and monopoly loss, must be determined with reference to particular agreements.

---

[241] Kaplow, *supra* note 219, at 1816.
[242] *Id*. at 1842.

First, Kaplow's test applies at the most specific level possible, such as licensing agreement. The input making up the ratio, patentee reward and monopoly loss, must be determined with reference to particular agreements. For instance, patentee reward and monopoly loss refer, respectively, to the incremental reward and loss resulting from the practice in question.[243] As Kaplow concedes, "various kinds of information needed for the analysis will not generally be available."[244] To ascribe particular numbers for patentee reward and monopoly loss and to arrive at ratios that dictate antitrust treatment of the practice is, admits Kaplow, "a most formidable and controversial endeavor."[245] If the project is this difficult for economists, it is impossible for counts. That no court has attempted to apply the test in eighteen years illustrates this this point. The test is limited to the level of the hypothetical theorem in seeking to analysis the composition of each elements of social welfare.[246]

Second, to the extent Kaplow offers a common denominator, it is total social welfare, such as it is offered economic welfare loss as a common denominator. The effect of an individual agreement on total welfare is determined by comparing the reward to the patentee with the monopoly loss resulting from the agreement.[247] Social welfare is a polycentric concept with numerous inputs, and Kaplow's version confronts hurdles in the interdependence among cases considered by court. He insists that courts "cannot hope to articulate a coherent patent-antitrust doctrine by proceeding on a case-by-case basis,"[248] because of the effects of each decision on related cases. In particular, "it is wholly indeterminate how any individual case or, similarly, any

---

[243] See Kaplow, *supra* note 219, at 1831-32.
[244] *Id.* at 1842.
[245] *Id.* at 1833.
[246] For example, in seeking to analyze the composition of each grain of sand on the beach of social welfare, rather than an approach that groups different sections of the beach with different characteristics (like white sand, gold sand, and rocks) into more assessable categories.
[247] *Id.* at 1831.
[248] *Id.* at 1844.

single component of patent-antitrust doctrine should be decided, because the question is whether the totality of the court's patent-antitrust decisions" promotes an appropriate level of reward.[249] Similarly, "setting the patent life and determining patent-antitrust doctrine are interdependent endeavors; in other words, the system of equations that defines the optimization process must be solved simultaneously."[250] By Kaplow, the task overlap because adjustments in patent-antitrust doctrine produce different levels of reward for any particular patent life, thus necessitating an adjustment of the optimal patent life.[251] He also explains that an adjustment in patent-antitrust doctrine leading to a greater reward ought to reduce the patent life.[252] The comprehensiveness of Kaplow's social welfare calculi limits their practical applicability.

Third, Kaplow's test seeks to maximize the reward to the patentee. Kaplow recognizes that patentee reward is not the end goal of the patent system, rather it is the means to increased inventive activity and benefits to society.[253] Kaplow stops at the level of patentee reward, however, because of the impossibility of proceeding further under his analysis. He cannot reach the stage of increased invention because he does not know "the identity of the patentee," in particular, the patentee's familiarity with the inventive process and specific antitrust restrictions.[254] And he cannot reach the ultimate stage of benefit to society because this is tied to the impracticable task of determining the optimal patent length. Thus, under Kaplow's analysis, the only end product to maximize is patentee reward. As he puts it, "fruitful analysis of the patent-antitrust problem may require the simplifying assumption that all reward has the same

---

[249] *Id.* at 1820.
[250] *Id.* at 1840.
[251] See *Id.* at 1839.
[252] This problem of the endless loop likely would apply even if a more narrow common denominator, such as innovation, were utilized.
[253] Kaplow, supra note 219, at 1823.
[254] *Id.* at 1839.

incentive effect."[255] However, cutting short the chain from patentee reward through inventive activity to benefit to society at the first step, shortchanges the objectives of the patent law. Patentee reward is not the objective of the patent system but is only a means to increase invention and innovation. Even if the elusive calculation of ultimate benefit to society cannot be made, the omission of the link between patentee reward and invention is disconcerting, particularly in industries in which patents are not critical to innovation.

Conclusion

The role of Empirical study in legal decision, even in the rule making, was increased by the economic development with the occurrence of economic realism. The incensement of economic implications of law, without exception, impacted to the court's ruling to antitrust cases and antitrust law-making itself. Now, as one of the common way, court uses concepts and theories developed by economists and weaves economic concepts into their judgement to support.

I believe that the classical perspective of economic theories regarding antitrust law was started from early theorist Adam Smith in 1776, even it denied the economic implication. Through this dissertation, it was examined several modern economic theories along with Posner's economic implication of antitrust law. Economic Realism, Neo-classical synthesis, and Chicago School's economic view on antitrust law also was covered briefly.

---

[255] *Id.*

In the same vein, as I discussed in Chapter II, economic concept becomes to play more significant role since the late 1970's. one of the example is the unavoidable tendencies from per se to rule of reason analysis in the U.S. Antitrust law. Moreover, the value of the pre se rule lost the merit unless pre-trial litigation does not have to address all rule of reason issues.

To analyze the substantial implication of economic theories, it should be back to Jefferson and Hamilton's contrasting views on governance. Because it is the same line with current debates on the antitrust law where we should put the value on protectionism for equality-enhancing opportunities or efficiency-enhancing competitions. Jefferson urged a deconcentrated society and government, one that valued independent decision-making and equality-enhancing opportunities for small, local business. Control of economic concentrations of industrial power was central to Jeffersonian populism. Hamilton, on the other hand, feared that decentralization might interfere with the goal of efficiency. He was an exponent of a strong national government, particularly central control over financial and economic issues and institutions.

Then, whether legal system and lawmakers should put the value on protectionism for equality-enhancing opportunities or efficiency-enhancing competitions. Throughout the discussion, it shows that under the antitrust law application, the alteration of legal methodology or doctrine specially in the antitrust law that the tendency of change from per se illegal application to rule of reason allocation, is an unavoidable tendency.

As a result, to analyze the case under the rule of reason standard, empirical economic data analysis plays siginificant role to support court's decision. The tendency of economic implication and increasing reliance of data analysis occurs the new risk of inequality of judicial discretions. Because economic data analysis needs experts' working with specialties on the relevant filed and statistic research and data analysis to be used to support the court decision. More significant problem is that it is very expensive process to produce the result of analysis. Moreover, the data analysis is easy to be contaminated by the person when the person has specific interests or biases. For example, when the economists conduct the statistical research, they usually conduct a survey that is one of the common analysis method in the statistic research. And when they make the survey questions, the wording in the survey questions can be contaminated by the person who conduct the survey with special interest or bias. How is the research settled depend on the experts and it can be impact to the result it-self. Thus, there is huge availability of risk that the result of economic analysis would be subjective and unfair.

I also discussed in Chapter III generally what is the economic approach in the legal regime as I explain the major economic theories, and why economic analysis is important tool in the field specially for the antitrust law, and how the court applied these economic implications specially in tying arrangement cases. Also, I showed that the importance of economic applications to antitrust law with previous court's decisions.

In Chapter IV, I discussed the confliction between IP and Antitrust through the cases. Louis Kaplow said that "as many commentators on the patent-antitrust intersection frame the issue as raising an inherent tension because antitrust aims to protect competition, whereas patent law creates monopolies that aim to eliminate competition in order to reward invention." However, my finding throughout in Chapter IV is that the conflict is not a real conflict that we generally or conceptually had been long-accepted. To support this idea, I introduced and criticized major modern economists' theories, such as William Baxter, Ward Bowman, and Louise Kaplow.

Ultimately, IP confliction issues with Antirust case should be analysis in the same line with the regular antitrust case analysis. It is not the matter of confliction between to protect competition and to eliminate competition, but the matter of alteration of legal application methodology or legal doctrine.

Thus, the Baxter's, Bowman's, and Kaplow's approaches each articulate thoughtful economic construct that address many of the difficult issues in the patent-antitrust intersection. But there is room for a new paradigm, not only because of the concerns discussed previously, but also because of weaknesses all three approaches share when applied to an examination of monopolists' patent-based actions.

First, all of the test poses substantial administrability problems. Economic approaches, with their seeming precision in theory, are helpful in ordering and weighing relevant factors but will often be extremely difficult to apply in practice. Not only are the particular inputs usually unmeasurable, but any calculation of ratios among these inputs quickly spirals out of the realm of plausibility. Compounding the problem is the recognition that it is courts that are charged with these tasks, which further diminishes the likelihood that such approaches will be adopted or effectively applied.

Second, none of the tests recognizes industry-specific differences that affect the achievement of social welfare. All three approaches reside simultaneously on a theoretical level and a specific, individualized level. As theoretical level, it exists in each argues from global understandings about the patent and antitrust systems, and as specific and individual level, it exists in determining the validity of particular agreements. However, a middle ground might offer benefits. An approach based on the relevant industry would recognize that the systems are not monolithic and would offer more hands-on, informed analyses. At the same time, it would solve many of the administrability problems by not descending to the level of particular practices.

Third, all three tests are designed to apply to licensing practices. Each orders relevant factors in analyzing the propriety of particular agreements. For instance, Kaplow applies his 'ratio' test to price-restricted licenses, patent combinations, price discrimination, and end-product royalty schemes. Also, Bowman's 'principal subject' consists of "the agreements that owners of patents make with others who wish to use them.[256] But such a paradigm only applies to a license, a completed agreement between patentee and licensee. Given that patentees may choose not to license at all, the question remains as to how courts should analyze a patentee's refusal to license.

Therefore, there is room for a new approach and the centerpiece of the new approach is an industry-specific analysis of innovation. The focusing of the new approach might anticipate several benefits.

First, it offers a common denominator. Innovation is the goal of the patent system and a critical objective of the antitrust laws. By endeavoring to increase innovation, the proposed test promises to take advantage of both the patent system and competition in those instance in which they have the most to contribute to innovation. The common denominator also offers courts an alternative to formalistic and incomplete tests based on the scope of the patent, the intent of the defendant, and the number of markets involved.

Second, it engages analysis at a productive level, so far unexplored, that is the level of industry. Commentators have offered approaches that simultaneously, 1) argue from global understandings about the patent and antitrust systems and, 2) apply on the narrow level of particular agreements. Such analyses neglect variations among industries and quickly bog down in impracticability.

The proposed rebuttable presumption offers a middle approach. It recognizes that the patent

---

[256] See *generally* Bowman, supra note 225.

and antitrust systems are not monolithic and that innovation takes place through different paths in different industries. For instance, patents are critical for innovation in the chemicals and pharmaceutical industries. Competitions is essential in industries in which network effects are significant, such as Internet business methods and computer software. The approach recognizes and orders the essential building blocks of the intersection that have until now been overlooked. The presence of market-based incentives to innovate, the ease of creating products, the difficulty of imitating products, and the cumulative path of innovation. At the same time, the test avoids severe administrability problems by not focusing exclusively on the level of particular practices, and it forges the otherwise impenetrable link between patentee reward and inventive activity.

Therefore, in acknowledging the incentives underlying the patent system while simultaneously preserving a role for the antitrust laws, the test concentrates the unique contributions of both systems in the attempt to increase innovation.

Finally, back to the role of Empirical study in legal decision, the alteration of legal methodology or doctrine specially in the antitrust law that the tendency of change of empirical data analyses and economic implications, is unavoidable. Economic data analysis can be another barrier for the party who has less availability to conduct expense data analyzing to support or to rebut the argument in the court. Thus, government should put resources or efforts to reduce the barriers that are producing unfair justice and inequalities.

Bibliography

\<Books\>

A. Berle, G. Means, The Modern Corporation and Private Property (1932).

A.D. Neal & D.G. Goyder, The Antitrust Laws of the U.S.A. (1980).

Adam Smith, An Inquiry into the Nature and Causes of the Wealth of Nation (1776).

Areeda, Phillip, Donald F. Turner, and Herbert Hovenkamp, Antitrust Law: An Analysis of Antitrust Principles and Their Application (1978)

E. Chamberlin, The Theory of Monopolistic Competition (1933).

Ethomas Sullivan & Jeffery L. Harrison, Understanding Antitrust and Its Economic Implication (2008)

F.M. Scherer, Industrial Market Structure and Economic Performance (1980).

Hans B. Thorelli, The Federal Antitrust Policy: Origination of an American Tradition (1954).

Henderson, Gerard Carl, The Federal Trade Commission: A Study in Administrative Law and Procedure (1924).

Herbert Hovenkamp, The Antitrust Enterprise: Principle and Execution (2005).

Ida M. Tarbell, The Hisotry of The Standard Oil Company/Ida M. Tarbell: Briefer version edited by David M. Chalmers (2003).

J. Robinson, The Economics of Imperfect Competition (1933).

K. Boulding, Economic Analysis (1941).

Legislative History and of the Powers, Duties and Procedures of the Commission (1915).

Levinson, Marc. The great A&P and the struggle for small business in America (2011).

Richard A. Posner, Antitrust Law: An Economic Perspective (1976).

Richard A. Posner, Economic Analysis of Law (1977).

Richard A. Posner, Frank H. Easterbrook, Antitrust (1981).

Richard A. Posner, The Economics of Justice (1983).

Saul Cornell, The Other Founders: Anti-federalism And the Dissenting Tradiion In America (1999).

Stephen M. Maurer, and Suzanne Scotchmer, The Essential Facilities Doctrine: The Lost Message of Terminal Railroad (2014).

Steve Fleetwood, Critical Realism in Economic: Development and Debate (1999).

Thomas L. Hayslett III, 1995 Antitrust Guidelines for the Licensing of Intellectual Property: Harmonizing the Commercial Use of Legal Monopolies with the Prohibition of Antitrust Law (1995).

Thomas R. Resale Price Maintenance: Economic Theories and Empirical Evidence (1984).

Ward Bowman, Patent and antitrust law: A legal and economic appraisal (1973).

\<Periodicals\>

[Law Journals]

Alan J. Messe, *Economic Theory Trader Freedom and Consumer Welfare: State Oil Co. v. Khan and the Continuing Incoherence of Antitrust Doctrine,* Cornell L. Rev. 84 (1998).

Areeda, Phillip, and Donald F. Turner. *Predatory pricing and related practices under Section 2 of the Sherman Act,* Harvard Law Review (1975).

Beckner, C. Frederick, and Steven C. Salop, *Decision theory and antitrust rules*, Antitrust Law Journal 67.1 (1999).

Bork, Robert H., *Legislative intent and the policy of the Sherman Act*, The Journal of Law and Economics 9 (1966).

Bork, Robert H., *The Rule of Reason and the Per Se Concept: Price Fixing and Market Division*, The Yale Law Journal 74.5 (1965).

Christopher OB. Wright, *The National Cooperative Research Act of 1984: A New Antitrust Regime for Joint Research and Development Ventures*, High Technology Law Journal 1.1 (1986).

Daniel R. Fischel, *Antitrust Liability for Attempts to Influence Government Action: The Basis and Limits of the Noerr-Pennington Doctrine*, The University of Chicago Law Review 45.1 (1977).

David B. Lytle, and Beverly Purdue, *Antitrust Target Area Under Section 4 of the Clayton Act: Determination of Standing in Light of the Alleged Antitrust Violation*, Am. UL Rev. 25 (1975).

Derek C. Bok, *Section 7 of the Clayton Act and the Merging of Law and Economics*, 74 Harv. L. Rev. 226, 233 (1960).

Earl W. Kinter, and Christopher Smith, *The Emergence of the Federal Trade Commission as a Formidable Consumer Protection Agency,* Mercer L. Rev. 26 (1974).

Flynn, John J., *Rethinking Sherman Act Section 1 Analysis: Three Proposals for Reducing the Chaos*, Antitrust Law Journal 49.4 (1980).

Frank M. *Machovec, Mises, Monopoly, and the Market Process*, 19 Cato J. 247, 258 (1999).

Handler, Milton, *Some Misadventures in Antitrust Policymaking. Nineteenth Annual Review,* The Yale Law Journal 76.1 (1966).

Gilbert Holland Montague, *Unfair Methods of Competition*, 25 Yale L.J. 20 (1915).

Herbert Hovenkamp, *The Sherman Act and the Classical Theory of Competition*, 74 Iowa L. Rev. 1019 (1989).

Hugh C. Hansen, *Robinson-Patman Law: A Review and Analysis,* Fordham L. Rev. 51 (1982).

James May, *Antitrust Practive and Procedure in the Formative Era: The Constitutional and Conceptual Reach of State Antitrust Law*, 1880-1918, 135 U. Pa. L. Rev. 495 (1987).

Louise Kaplow, *The Patent Antitrust Intersection: A Reappraisal,* 97 HARV. L. REV. 1813 (1984).

Milton Handler, *Changing Trends in Antitrust Doctrines: An Unprecedented Supreme Court Term—1977,* Columbia Law Review 77.7 (1977).

Neil W. Averitt, *The Meaning of Unfair Methods of Competition in Section 5 of the Federal Trade Commission Act*, BcL REv. 21 (1979).

Petrowitz, Harold C., *Federal Court Reform: The Federal Courts Improvement Act of 1982--And Beyond*, Am. UL Rev. 32 (1982).

Richard A. Posner, *The rule of reason and the economic approach: Reflections on the Sylvania decision,* The University of Chicago Law Review 45.1 (1977).

Richard A. Posner, *The Federal Trade Commission: A Retrospective*, 72 Antitrust L.J. 761, 765 (2005).

Robert H. Bork, *Legislative intent and the Policy of the Sherman Act*, 9 J.L. & Econ. 7, 37 (1966).

Robert H. Bork, *The Rule of Reason and the Per & Concept. Price Fixing and Market Division,* 75 YALE LJ..373 (1966)

Robert H Landes & Richard A. Posner, *Market Power in Antitrust Cases* 94 Harv. L. Rev. 937 (1981).

Robert H. Lande*, Wealth Transfers as the Original and Primary Concern of Antitrust: The Efficiency Interpretation Challenged*, 34 Hastings L.J. 65, 68-70 (1982).

Robert Pitofsky, *Antitrust and intellectual property: unresolved issues at the heart of the new economy,* Berk. Tech. LJ 16 (2001).

Stephen Calkins, *California Dental Association: Not a quick look but not the full Monty,* Antitrust Law Journal 67.3 (2000).

Stephen W. Gard, *Purpose and Promise Unfulfilled: A Different View of Private Enforcement Under the Federal Trade Commission Act*, Nw. UL Rev. 70 (1975).

William F. Baxter*, Legal Restrictions on Exploitation of the Patent Monopoly: An Economic Analysis*, 76 YALE L.J. 267, at 313 (1966)

113

William L. Letwin, *Congress and the Sherman Antitrust Law: 1887-1890*, 23 U.Chi.L.Rev 221 (1956).

[Other Journals]

Bourdieu, Pierre, *A reasoned utopia and economic fatalism*, New Left Review 227 (1998).

Carlos D. Ramirez, and Christian Eigen-Zucchi, *Understanding the Clayton Act of 1914: An analysis of the interest group hypothesis*, Public Choice 106.1-2 (2001).

Dennis C. Mueller, *Merger policy in the United States: a reconsideration,* Review of Industrial Organization 12.5-6 (1997).

Donald J. Boudreaux, *The second edition of Judge Posner's Antitrust Law: A tempered appreciation,* The Antitrust Source (2002).

Lerner Index can be found in Abba Lerner, *The concept of Monopoly and the Measurement of Monopoly Power*, 1 Rev. Econ. Stud. 157 (1934).

Levi, Edward H, The Parke, *Davis-Colgate Doctrine: The Ban on Resale Price Maintenance,* The Supreme Court Review 1960 (1960).

Stephen A. Rhoades, *The Herfindahl-Hirschman Index*, Fed. Res. Bull. 79 (1993).

Thomas E. Sullivan, *The Antitrust Division as a Regulatory Agency: An Enforcement Policy in Transition,* Wash. ULQ 64 (1986): 997.

<Cases>

Arizona v. Maricopa County Medical Society, 457 U.S. 332, 102 S.Ct. 2466 (1982).

Broadcast Music, Inc. v. Columbia Broadcasting System, Inc. (BMI), 441 U.S. 1, 99 S.Ct. 1551 (1979).

California Dental Assn. v. FTC, 526 U.S. 756, 119 S.Ct. 1604 (1999).

Continental T.V., Inc. v. GTE Sylvania, Inc., 433 U.S. 36 (1977).

Eastman Kodak Co. v. Image Technical Servs., 504 U.S. 451 (1992).

FTC v. British Oxygen Co., 529 F.2d 196 (3d Cir. 1976).

FTC v. Cardinal Health, Inc., 12 F. Supp. 2d 34 (D.D.C. 1998).

FTS v. Dean foods Co., 384 U.S. 597 (1966).

FTC v. Elders Grain, Inc., 868 F.2d 901(7th Cir. 1989).

FTC v. Indiana Federation of Dentists, 476 U.S. 447 (1986).

FTC v. Merchant Servs. Direct, LLC, 2013 Trade Cas.

FTC v. Whole Foods Mkt., Inc., 548 F.3d 1028 (D.C. Cir. 2008);

Holloway v. Bristo-Myers Corp., 485 F.2d 986 (D.C. Cir. 1973).

Illinois Tool Works, Inc. v. Independent Ink, Inc., 547 U.S. 28 (2006).

International Salt Co. v. United States, 332 U.S. 392 (1947)

Jacob Siegel Co v. FTC, 327 U.S. 608 (1946).

Jeter v. Credit Bureau, Inc., 754 F.2d 907 (11th Cir. 1985)

National Athletic Ass's v. Board of Regents of the University of Oklahoma, 468 U.S. 85 (1984).

National Society of Professional Engineers v. United States, 435 U.S. 679, 98 S.Ct. 1355 (1978).

Planned Parenthood v. Casey, 505 U.S. 833 (1992).

Standard Oil Co. v. United States, 221 U.S. 1 (1911).

State Oil Co. v. Khan, 552 U.S. 3, 20 (1997).

United States v. A. Schrader's Son, 252 US 85 (1920).

United States v. Colgate & Co., 250 U.S. 300 (1919).

<Others>

US LEGAL, Inc., https://definitions.uslegal.com/p/per-se-rule/ (last

www.ingramcontent.com/pod-product-compliance
Lightning Source LLC
Chambersburg PA
CBHW081133170526

45165CB00008B/2655